Crafts

for

Kids

A Month-by-Month
Idea Book

2nd Edition

BARBARA L. DONDIEGO
ILLUSTRATED BY JACQUELINE CAWLEY

TAB Books
Division of McGraw-Hill

New York San Francisco Washington, D.C. Auckland Bogotá
Caracas Lisbon London Madrid Mexico City Milan
Montreal New Delhi San Juan Singapore
Sydney Tokyo Toronto

To my wonderful husband, Dan, and to my children,
Terry, Barbara, Elizabeth, and Mary.

pbk 6 7 8 9 10 11 12 13 14 DOC/DOC 9 9 8 7 6
hc 1 2 3 4 5 6 7 8 9 DOH/DOH 9 9 8 7 6 5 4 3 2 1 0

Library of Congress Cataloging-in-Publication Data

Dondiego, Barbara L.
    Crafts for kids : a month-by-month idea book / by Barbara L.
  Dondiego.—2nd ed.
      p.   cm.
      Includes index.
      ISBN 0-8306-7573-6 (h)   ISBN 0-8306-3573-4 (p)
      1. Handicraft. I. Title.
    TT157.D63   1990
    745.5—dc20   90-37849
                                                  CIP

Acquisitions Editor: Kimberly Tabor
Book Editor: Joanne M. Slike
Director of Production: Katherine G. Brown
Photography by Nicholas Cole Photography, 258 Cole Street, Marietta, GA 30060

Contents

Acknowledgments

I would like to thank the beautiful children who posed for the photography in this book. They are: Barbara Dondiego, Elizabeth Dondiego, Mary Dondiego, Jennifer Wright, Ashley Berry, Albert Berry, Clark Berry, Mark Doucette, Carrie Cohen, Aaron Cohen, Diane Isaacson, Jennifer Levine, Amy Takahashi, Eric Takahashi, John Cole, Mary Loretta Cole, Jean-Paul Fournier, Christina Fournier, Jennifer Geller, and Melanie Phelps.

The helping parents who posed with their children are: Louis Cohen, Nancy Berry, Pam Cole, and Mike Doucette.

A portion of the photography was taken in Chestnut Ridge Day School, and I would like to thank Les Cole and Kirsten Asta for allowing me to use their building. The classroom scenes were shot at Primrose Country Day School. I would like to thank Paul and Marcy Erwin and Linda Sabol for making these pictures possible.

Introduction

This is a handbook of Craft-training, a method of teaching preschool skills. When children up to age 12 use this book, they learn to be creative with the things around them. All ages can learn advanced construction techniques as they measure, fringe, pleat, curl, and glue.

Craft-training prepares children to participate in school without taking the place of school. It teaches children preschool skills methodically and purposefully, while showing them how to create with craft materials that are inexpensive and easy to find. The children end each craft session with an interesting and often decorative product, and with a better understanding of the preschool skills emphasized by the craft. The crafts themselves are precisely written, with suggestions for what the adult can say to the child to teach particular skills. The realistic illustrations will help you guide children to successful completed projects.

There are two big differences between this craft book and others on the market. First, these crafts are inexpensive. Most of them are made from things that can be found in the supermarket and drugstore. The school and office supplies sections of these stores yield everything from scissors and glue to permanent markers. Pipe cleaners are found in the smoking section. Flour for paste and for flour-salt dough is probably already in your kitchen cupboard. In other words, you do not need to raid an expensive craft store to interest your children in crafts. Movable, paste-on eyes and flexible strip magnets are used for several of the crafts, but they are rarely needed and are used simply because the children can make a different type of craft with them. To purchase these items you must go to a craft store and ask for them by name. The eyes come in packets of eight or more, and the magnets come on a large roll which can be cut with scissors. You will have enough of each to make several craft items.

The second thing that makes this book unique is that it is a handbook for Craft-training, a new idea for teaching children the skills they need to succeed in school.

While making a craft, the child cuts with scissors, colors and pastes neatly, and paints with a brush. He counts and is repeatedly exposed to shapes, letters, sizes, and colors. As he manipulates the craft materials, he develops eye-hand coordination, which is the ability to make his hands and fingers do the things that his eyes want them to do. This skill is very important when the child learns writing and math. (Any adult who has tried to thread a needle can understand what eye-hand coordination is!)

As the child talks about the craft with an adult, he develops precise language skills, also important to school success. As he assembles the craft with an adult's guidance, he learns to listen, to follow directions, and to think and act in sequence. He knows the joy of sitting still long enough to make something himself. Children display their creations with great pride because they make them with their own hands.

Children as young as 2 years can begin Craft-training. By the time they enter kindergarten, they will have mastered the skills they need to succeed in school.

Each craft is presented with a list of materials needed to make the craft, a list of skills that can be taught with the craft, and exact instructions showing you how to teach it. Keywords that should be said to the child are *in italics*. Words such as *orange triangle* and *three white circles* are repeated in the natural process of making the craft. Without memorizing or being formally taught, the child will learn the skills needed for school, and you will be his teacher.

The cooking projects were included in this book for a very special reason. A child who is very active and physical and is on the go every minute of the day, is a child who could benefit a great deal from Craft-training, since schools will expect him to behave in a controlled manner. They will expect him to have an adequate attention span, to listen without interrupting, and to follow simple directions in order. Yet he may take no interest whatsoever in working with crafts if it means that he must sit still, listen, and follow directions for a few minutes. The best way that I have found to get his attention is with cooking activities. He will always be interested in eating, especially if the food is particularly yummy. When he discovers that he must participate in the making of the food project in order to eat his portion, his attention and cooperation increase dramatically.

When working with food, of course, he is immediately rewarded for his effort. He gets to consume his craft. This positive experience will be useful after a few craft sessions. It won't be long before he will happily work on nonfood crafts as well. Instead of eating it, he will show it off. This carry-over is sometimes the only way that you will gain a child's cooperative effort, and you can always go back to using edible crafts if the child's interest wanes.

By making the crafts in this book with an adult's help, a preschooler can learn:

- How to hold a pencil properly for writing
- How to color "within the lines"
- How to read his first and last name
- How to print his first name, using capital and lowercase letters
- How to recognize numbers up to 10
- How to count out loud up to 20
- How to follow directions given by an adult
- How to think and act in sequence, such as "First we do this. Next we do this."
- How to cut neatly with scissors
- How to paste and glue neatly, without eating the paste
- How to draw a recognizable person
- How to paint with a brush without mixing up all the colors
- The names of the five basic shapes: square, circle, triangle, rectangle, and diamond
- The names of all basic colors: red, yellow, blue, orange, green, purple, black, white, brown, and pink

With Craft-training, children will learn the basic skills needed for school success, but they will not realize they are being taught. By following the directions outlined in each project, any adult can be a teacher. It's fun; it's easy, and it will give your child a head start in learning school skills.

How to Teach Your Child by Making Crafts

1. Set aside an hour 5 days a week to create crafts with your child. If he can invite a friend to join him, it will be even more fun.

2. Let him pick out the craft he wants to make.

3. Check the Materials List for the craft. Buy what is needed. Also buy a package of tracing paper. It can be found in the school and office supplies section of grocery stores and drugstores.

4. Follow the directions for making the craft. It is very important to encourage your child to do as much of the work of making the craft as he possibly can. The more he cuts, the better he will get at it. The more he is told to hold his marker or crayon "the right way," the more accustomed to writing he will become. Learning preschool skills is truly a case of "practice makes perfect."

5. Talk to your child while he makes the craft. Tell him that the cardboard roll used to make the Totem Pole is a *cylinder*, for instance. Tell him that the bat is *nocturnal* and that it uses *echolocation* to catch insects at night. In this way he will build knowledge and vocabulary as well as increasing coordination skills for his eyes, hands, and fingers.

6. Praise your child for what he has created!

January

The projects in this chapter are perfect for chilly January evenings. Children can make such projects as the Balloon Man or the Cylinder Snowman at the kitchen table while you keep an eye on supper. Except for watercolor painting, which can drag on for an hour or so, each craft takes only a few minutes of your time and very little of your money.

Eye-Hand Coordination & Small Motor Skills

The skills children will learn by making these crafts are basic. Everyone should learn them as early as possible. During every craft, the children make their eyes, hands, and fingers work together. These skills are called "eye-hand coordination" and "small motor skills." At school, a child must follow words with his eyes to learn reading and must copy letters and figures onto a paper to write, so these abilities are very important. If you help him practice eye-hand coordination and small motor skills at as young an age as possible, he will grow amazingly adept at them.

"Large motor skills," incidentally, are being practiced when children climb, run, jump down the stairs, fall over furniture, slide down the railing, leap through the hallway, and generally drive you crazy by being in the house all winter.

The next time your child is acting in such a manner, and you want to sound particularly knowledgeable, just scream, "Jimmy, will you please stop practicing your large motor skills!" It may not be a very effective way to calm him down, but at least you will give the impression of being in control of the situation.

Craft-Training Skills to Learn

The crafts in this chapter do not have to be done in any order. Select one that interests you and your child, check the Materials List to see if you have the necessary items on hand, and approach it with the idea that you are going to use that craft to teach your child the school-related skills listed with it.

Craft-training skills to practice in January include:

- Learning the names of colors
- How to glue
- How to read his or her name
- How to print his or her name
- How to use paints
- How to draw a face
- Learning basic geometric shapes
- Counting to 10
- Learning the meaning of *under*, *on top of*, *inside*, and *a pair*
- Learning to use descriptive words
- How to cut. ("Practice makes perfect," you know; so don't be afraid to give your 2-year-old rounded safety scissors. Just don't let him cut his hair—or his brother's.)

BALLOON MAN

When the children are getting restless cooped up inside on dreary January days, let Balloon Man come to your rescue (FIG. 1-1). He will provide safe indoor play as the children use their muscle power to throw him around. No matter how he is tossed about, he always lands on his feet.

Skills to Teach

Teach children 2 years old and up:

- The color of the balloon
- How to read his or her name
- How to draw a face

Teach children 5 years old and up:

- How to blow up and tie a balloon
- How to cut out feet

Materials List

- A 9-inch balloon for each Balloon Man
- Construction paper of lightweight cardboard
- Scissors
- Permanent markers
- Transparent tape

1-1 The Balloon Man

Directions

Let each child choose a balloon. Emphasize the balloon's color. Say, "What color balloon do you want, Mary?" Mary does not know her colors, so she does not say anything. She points to a balloon. "Do you want a *red* one? Here is a *round, red* balloon for you." Give Mary the balloon.

Blow up the balloon for everyone who cannot do it. Tie the end in a fat knot.

Cut out a foot for each Balloon Man by tracing the pattern in FIG. 1-2. Children 5 years old and up can cut their own if you draw it for them. Have them draw toes or shoelaces on the foot.

Insert the balloon's knot in CUT A of the foot, so that the knot is on the bottom. A small piece of tape will hold the cut shut so the knot will not pop out.

Using permanent markers, each child should draw a face on his or her own balloon. Closely supervise the children when they use permanent markers because the markers stain.

Print the child's name on the back of the Balloon Man's head. Use both uppercase and lowercase letters. The children will read their own names and find their own particular balloon's color each time they throw the balloons around.

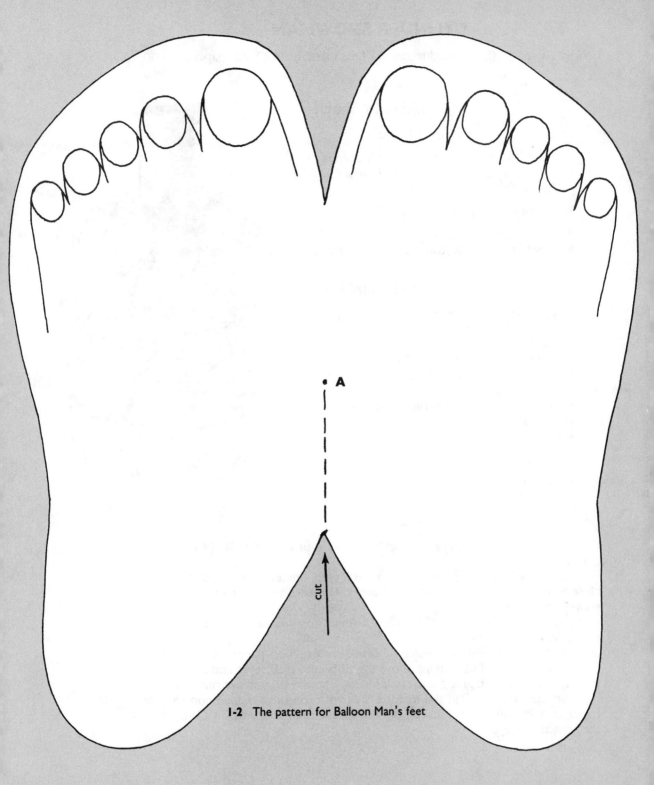

A

cut

1-2 The pattern for Balloon Man's feet

CYLINDER SNOWMAN

He's so fat and fluffy it's hard to believe he's made from a toilet paper roll (FIG. 1-3)!

Skills to Teach

Teach children 4 years old and up:

- The *cylinder*, *rectangle*, and *circle* shapes
- The meaning of *large* and *small*, *above* and *below*
- How to fold a circle *in half*

Teach children 6 years old and up:

- The meaning of *one-third*
- How to make a hat from two circles and a rectangle

Materials List

- Newspapers to cover work area
- A milk lid to fill with glue
- A toilet paper roll
- Cotton balls (cosmetic puffs), about 40
- Two pieces of 22-inch long yarn or narrow ribbon, in any color
- Black and orange construction paper
- Scissors
- Glue
- Ruler
- Pencil
- Paper punch

1-3 The Cylinder Snowman

Directions

Cover the work area with newspaper and give your child a milk lid filled with glue.

Tell the child to dip cotton balls into the glue, one at a time, and stick them close together on the outside of the *cylinder*. He should cover the cylinder completely with cotton.

Help him tie two pieces of ribbon in a single bow *one-third* of the way down the *cylinder*.

Use the paper punch to make 12 black construction paper circles. Tell the child to glue some of the circles *above* the ribbon to make eyes and a mouth for the snowman. He can glue some circles *below* the ribbon to make buttons.

Use the pattern in FIG. 1-4 to trace a carrot nose onto orange construction paper, then cut out. The child can dip the wide end in glue and stick it between the snowman's eyes.

To make the hat: Use the pattern in FIG. 1-4 to draw a 1³/₄-×-5¹/₂-inch rectangle on black construction paper. Then draw a large and small black circle, again using the pattern. Cut these out. Help the child roll the rectangle into a cylinder 1³/₄ inches tall and glue it so it holds its shape. Set aside to dry.

Tell the child to fold the *large circle in half.* Starting in the middle of the folded edge, he should make a ³/₄-inch cut, straight up. Open the circle. He should fold it again, but this time, have him fold it on the cut. Again starting in the middle of the folded edge, make another ³/₄-inch cut, straight up. When he opens the circle, the two cuts should make a plus sign in the middle of it. This is the hat brim.

The cuts form four triangles in the middle of the hat brim. Tell the child to bend the triangles upward. He should apply glue to the outside of each triangle.

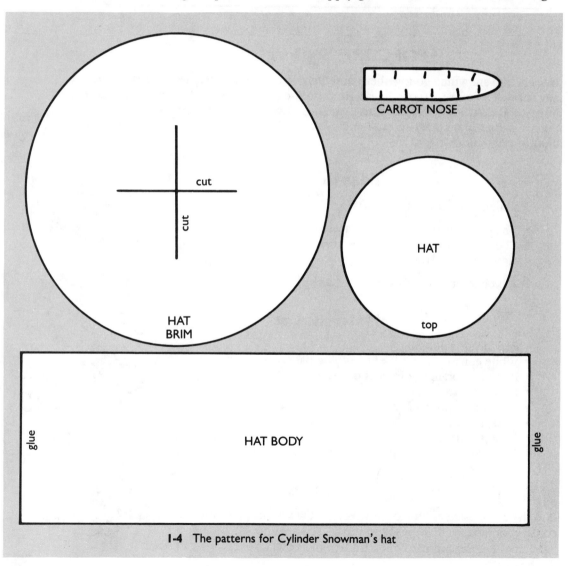

1-4 The patterns for Cylinder Snowman's hat

Slip the cylinder over the four triangles of the hat brim. The child can use his fingers to press the triangles against the inside of the cylinder. The triangles will try to come loose, but he should keep pressing on each one until the glue begins to dry and stick.

Tell the child to put glue on the top edge of the cylinder with his finger. Then he can place the *small circle* on the cylinder to finish the hat.

He can put glue on the top of the snowman's head, and lay the hat on it.

woolie-pullie

Give each child a milk lid for easy one-finger gluing. Fill the lid with glue. When craft time is over, let the lid dry. Use it again and again.

POPCORN SNOWMAN

January and snowmen go together naturally, even if you live where there is never any snow. Of course, a 2- or 3-year old cannot cut out a very good circle; so you must cut the shapes before the activity begins. When young children put together precut shapes, they practice eye-hand coordination, and they have an attractive craft to call their own (FIG. 1-5).

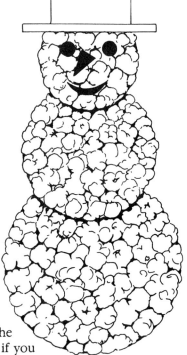

1-5 Popcorn Snowman

Skills to Teach

Teach children 2 years old and up:

- The colors *white*, *red*, *black*, and *orange*
- The *circle*, *triangle*, *square*, and *rectangle* shapes
- How many make *3*

Teach children 4 years old and up cutting skills.

Materials List

- Popcorn for popping
- White construction paper or typing paper
- Black and orange construction paper
- Nontoxic white glue
- Milk lids to put glue in
- Scissors
- Table salt (optional)
- Extra construction paper, any color

Directions

Pop the corn, using as little oil as possible. Oil will seep out into the construction paper if you use too much, so use a hot-air popper if you have one. Put the unsalted popcorn in a big bowl so everyone can reach it.

Draw three circles of graduated sizes on white paper for each snowman; you can use the patterns in FIGS. 1-6 and 1-7. If you plan to make several Popcorn Snowmen, stack the white papers together, staple them, and cut several shapes at one time.

Using the patterns, trace the square "top of hat," the rectangle "brim of hat," and two circle eyes onto black paper. Trace the triangle nose onto orange paper, and the mouth onto red paper.

Children 4 years old and up can cut their own shapes. Cut them out for younger children before the craft session begins. Don't expect the children to sit and watch you cut out shapes for 10 minutes. They will eat all the popcorn and then run off to play.

Pour a small amount of white glue into a jar lid for each child. Be sure to use nontoxic glue in case the children decide to have a snack while making this craft.

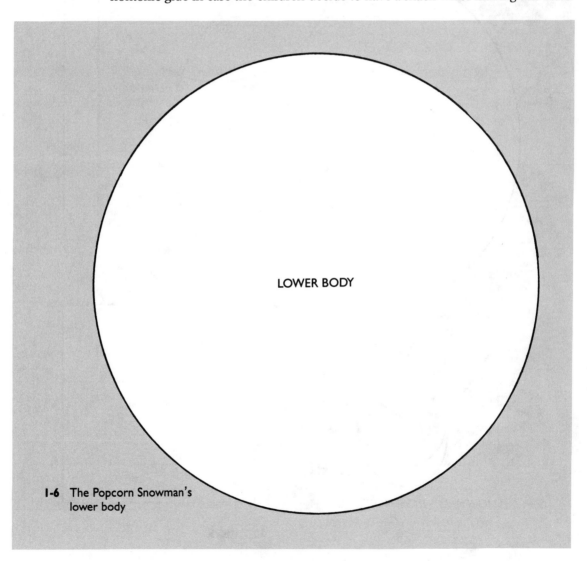

LOWER BODY

1-6 The Popcorn Snowman's lower body

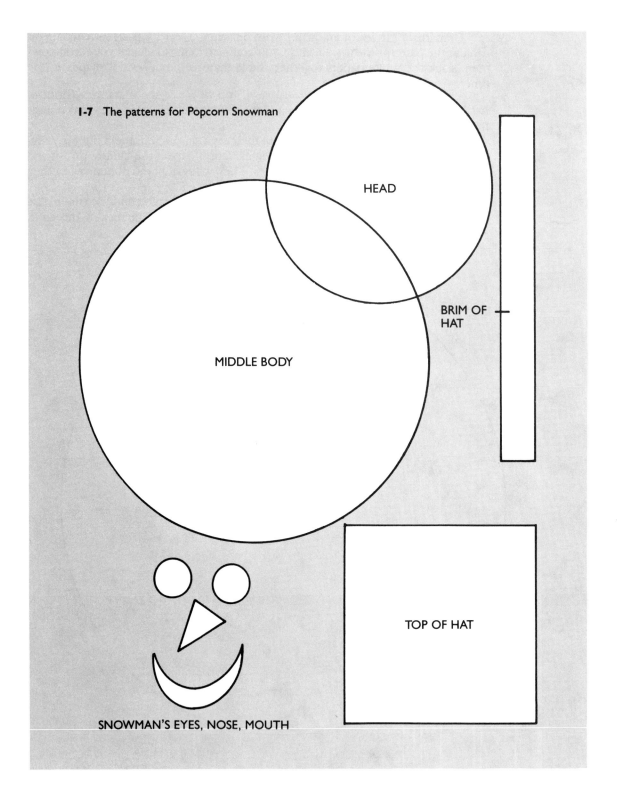

1-7 The patterns for Popcorn Snowman

HEAD

BRIM OF HAT

MIDDLE BODY

TOP OF HAT

SNOWMAN'S EYES, NOSE, MOUTH

Give each child all the shapes he will need to make the snowman. Then tell the children the following: "Glue the *three white circles* onto the piece of construction paper so that they make a snowman. Use the *large circle* for the snowman's bottom, the *middle-sized circle* for the snowman's middle, and the *small circle* for the head." Help each child to do it correctly so the snowman is not laying down sideways or standing on his head.

Tell them to put the *black rectangle* about one-third of the way down the snowman's head for a hat brim. Then they can glue the *black square above* the brim to complete the hat.

Show the children how to dip each piece of popcorn in the glue and stick it on the circles. They can continue to do this step until the snowman is covered or until they get tired. No matter how they do it, the craft will look pretty good.

Tell the children to glue on the *two black circle* eyes, the *orange triangle* nose, and the *red* mouth.

A background can be added with crayons. If you want to get really fancy, brush white glue on the background and cover it with table salt. Shake off the excess and let it dry for a sparkly effect.

When you display the Popcorn Snowman, tape it up high or the children will try to eat it.

_____ woolie-pullie _____

Count everything out loud. After awhile it will become such a habit that you will find yourself counting even when no child is around!

Count stairs as you go up or down.
How many kisses to erase a frown.
Count buttons as you fasten his jacket.
How many shushes to quiet their racket.
("That's ONE!")
Count bites of peas upon her plate.
Before you know it, they'll be counting great!

WATERCOLOR PAINTING

Painting with watercolors is a lot of fun for children and needn't be hard on you. I know many mothers who will not buy their children paints, markers, scissors, and glue because they can't stand messes. This doesn't have to be the case. Just pull up long sleeves and put a paint smock on everyone; a large shirt turned backwards works fine.

Skills to Teach

Teach children 2 years old and up:

- The names of colors
- How to read his or her name
- How to paint without mixing up the colors

Materials List

- Old newspapers to cover the kitchen table
- A watercolor paint set and a brush for each child
- Cups or bowls for rinse water. (Choose ones that do not tip easily.)
- White paper. (I use discarded computer paper. If you
  know anyone who is a secretary, see if you can get
  discarded typing paper, or buy plain white paper.)

Directions

Lay down several thicknesses of newspaper on your kitchen table. Lay down some ground rules for the children, too, such as: "Paint the paper only. If you paint yourself, your neighbor, or the walls, you will lose your right to paint forevermore. Do not get out of your seat and change your own rinse water. In fact, do not get out of your seat at all until I can help you." With these simple rules, everyone can enjoy being an artist.

Show the children how to rub a wet brush on the paint and transfer the color to their paper. Show them how to rinse their brushes so that the colors do not mix together.

Comment on their paintings by saying, "What a nice *red* (or whatever color they are using) design," or "I like your painting, I see that you're using *purple* ."

You can also emphasize painting skills and colors by saying to a particular child, "Mary, let's use *yellow* this time." Hold Mary's hand and help her swish her brush in the yellow paint. Then let her paint with this brush full of yellow.

If a child can sit in a high chair, he can paint. Put a bib on the child and tape a piece of painting paper to the high chair tray. Fasten a set of watercolors to the tray by rolling up two or three pieces of tape and sticking them on the bottom of the paint set. Add a little bit of water to all the colors—a pump sprayer, such as an old hair spray or window cleaner bottle filled with water, is handy for this. Give the child a brush and show him how to dip into the paints. Take away his painting as soon as he is finished, and let him get down as soon as he is bored. Do not give him rinse water unless you plan to mop the floor that day.

One word of caution: adults feel most comfortable when children paint things that we can recognize. Children just like to paint. Try not to say, "What is it?" when you look at their creations.

Snowy day pictures look really special if glitter is added to the picture. Brush on white glue and pour on glitter. Shake the excess glitter onto waxed paper and return it to the glitter bottle. You can often find glitter in the drugstore if no craft store is nearby. Even a 2-year-old's smudges can be titled "A Snowy Day" if glitter is added.

woolie-pullie

White chalk shows up great on black paper. The children can draw snowmen, snowy scenes, or falling snow. Spray with artist's fixative, which you can find in a craft store, or with hairspray so the chalk will not rub off easily.

FISHBOWL

The fishbowl is a delight for children to both make and display (FIG. 1-8). The rice and shells give it a three-dimensional effect.

Skills to Teach

Teach children 2 years old and up:

- The colors *blue*, *orange*, and *white*
- The meaning of *on top of*
- To count to *10*
- Gluing skills
- How to print his or her name

Teach children 4 years old and up cutting skills.

Materials List

- Blue and white construction paper
- Orange construction paper
- Rice
- Small shell macaroni
- Scissors
- Glue

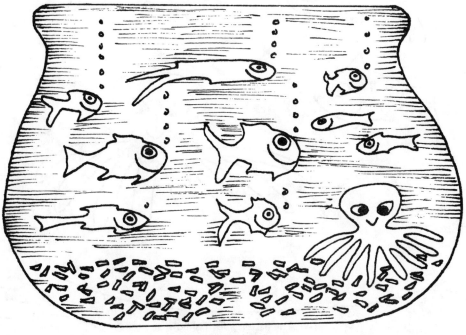

I-8 The Fishbowl

Directions

For each child, use the pattern in FIG. 1-9 to trace the fishbowl in the middle of the white paper. Carefully cut it out. Children 4 years old and up should cut their own. Keep the paper outline of the bowl and discard the cutout.

Trace on orange paper and cut out a set of 10 fish for each child. Let the older children cut their own. As you give each child his set of *ten orange* fish, count the fish together, out loud.

1-9 The patterns for Fishbowl and fish

Tell the children to glue the *white* paper that has the fishbowl outline, *on top of* the *blue* paper so the edges of the papers are even. This "fills" the fishbowl with *blue* "water."

Tell the children to glue grains of rice on the bottom of the fish bowl to make "sand" by squirting glue on the picture, piling rice on the glue and shaking off the excess. Then they can add "seashells" by gluing on shell macaroni.

Tell the children to glue their *ten orange* fish in the bowl, counting out loud as they glue.

Make sure each child prints his or her name on the finished picture so that everyone can tell who made it. Hold his hand lightly if necessary so that he holds the pencil correctly and writes the uppercase and lowercase letters neatly.

woolie-pullie

Turtles and frogs spend January hibernating in the mud or under warm leaves. This is a good time of year for a nature lesson, even if you can't go outside. Visit your library with the children and find books about animals in winter. Read or tell the children stories about the animals.

PAPER PLATE FROG

The very cheapest white generic paper plates make wonderful material for artwork, such as this Paper Plate Frog (FIG. 1-10). They do not have a design to interfere with your craft and they are not heavily waxed, which makes it easy to color on them with crayons and markers. (Just don't serve macaroni and cheese on them.)

Skills to Teach

Teach children 2 years old and up:

- The colors *white* and *green*
- How many make *2* and how many make *4*
- How to print his or her name

Teach children 4 years old and up:

- Cutting and gluing skills
- The meaning of *under*, *on top of*, and *inside*

Materials List

- A plain white paper plate for each child
- Green construction paper
- Crayons
- Scissors
- Glue

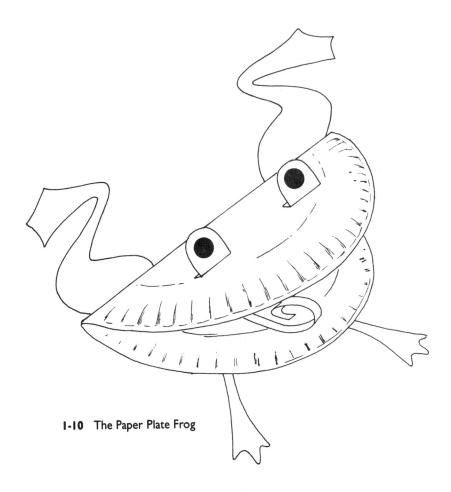

1-10 The Paper Plate Frog

Directions

Help each child fold a *white* paper plate in half to make the frog's body and mouth combined.

Use the pattern in FIG. 1-11 to trace two back legs and two front legs onto green construction paper for each frog. Cut these shapes out for your smaller child; encourage children 4 years old and up to cut their own. Have tape handy for mending, because it's hard for children to cut skinny frog arms and toes.

Trace two eyes onto green paper. The children can cut them out and draw eyeballs on them.

Make a long tongue so the frog can catch flies. Cut a strip of green construction paper 1/4 × 8 inches for each frog. Curl it tightly around a pencil, and remove the pencil.

Tell the children to glue *four green* legs *under* the frog's body. Tell them to glue the *two green* eyes *on top of* the frog's head so that they stick up. Tell them to glue the *green* curled tongue *inside* the frog's mouth.

The children can color the frogs with *green* crayons. They can color the inside of the mouth red or green and can draw *two* dots for his nose.

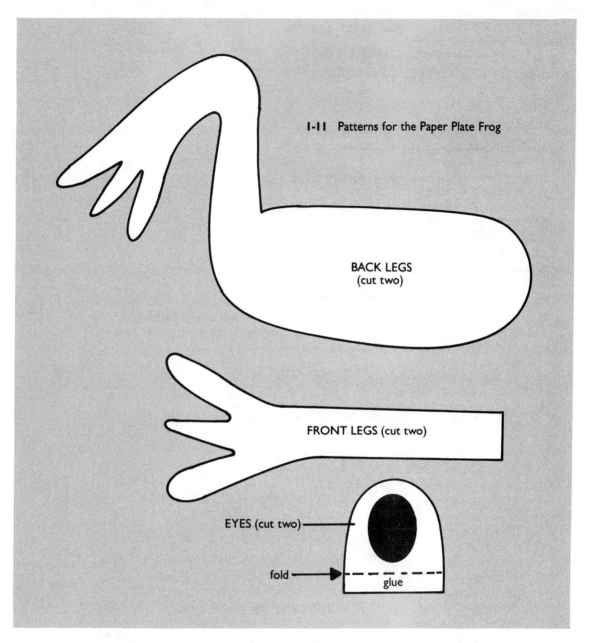

1-11   Patterns for the Paper Plate Frog

BACK LEGS
(cut two)

FRONT LEGS (cut two)

EYES (cut two)

fold

glue

Each person should print his or her name on the bottom of his frog. Make sure the children hold their crayons correctly for coloring or writing, and that they use uppercase and lowercase letters in their name.

PAPER PLATE TURTLE

Another project that uses paper plates is the Paper Plate Turtle (FIG. 1-12).

Skills to Teach

Teach children 2 years old and up:

- The colors *white*, *green*, and *brown*
- How many make *4*
- Gluing skills
- Coloring skills

Teach children 4 years old and up cutting skills.

Materials List

- 9-inch paper plates
- Green construction paper
- Green and brown crayons
- Scissors
- Glue

Directions

For each turtle, trace and cut out four feet, a pointed tail, and a head from green paper (FIG. 1-13). Children 4 years old and up can cut out their own if you draw them first.

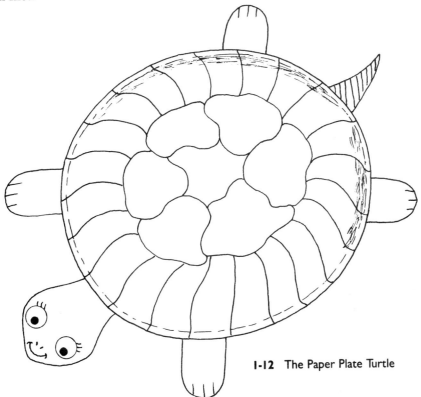

1-12   The Paper Plate Turtle

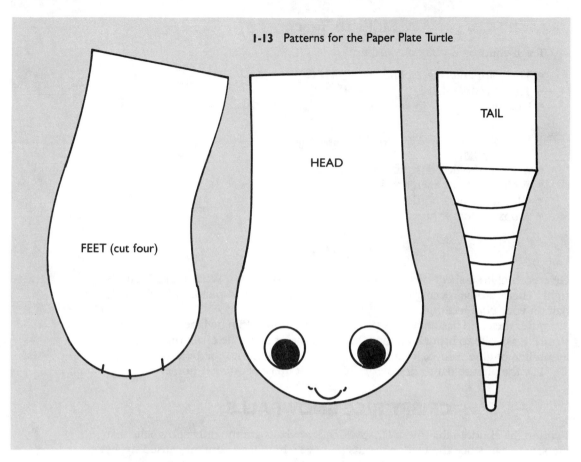

Show the children how to decorate the *bottom* of the paper plate to resemble a turtle shell, using *green* and *brown* crayons. You might want to draw the shell design on the plate for younger children, and let them color it.

Tell the children to glue the *four green* feet to the underside of the turtle's shell. Tell them to glue the *green* head and *green* tail to the underside, also.

As soon as his turtle dries, each child can draw eyes, nose holes, and a mouth on the turtle's head with crayons. Then he can turn the turtle over and print his name on the underside of the shell. Help the children hold their crayons correctly when coloring and writing.

SALT PICTURES

Making Salt Pictures is an easy way to teach children about winter and help them practice their drawing skills. The children simply draw a chalk picture and cover it with salt.

Skills to Teach

Teach children 2 years old and up:

- The colors *blue* and *white*
- The *rectangle* shape
- Drawing skills

Materials List

- A sheet of blue construction paper for each child
- White chalk for each child
- Glue in a squirt bottle
- A box to dump the salt into

Directions

Give each child a sheet of construction paper as you say, "What is this? That's right. This is a blue rectangle. Use the *white chalk* to draw a picture of a winter's day on your *blue rectangle*."

After the child has drawn his picture (even scribbles can be labeled "A Snowstorm"), ask him to bring it to you. Outline some or all of the chalk drawing with a thin line of glue. Pour salt on it. Dump the excess salt into the box.

Lay the picture flat to dry before hanging it up or sending it home.

CRISPY RICE SNOWBALLS

Remind the children that these Crispy Rice Snowballs are the only snowballs that are safe to eat, since the real ones outside have a high lead content caused by air pollution (FIG. 1-14).

Skills to Teach

Teach children 2 years old and up:

- To sit still, listen, and follow directions
- To count to *9*
- How to read his or her name
- To use words such as *sticky, crisp, firmly,* and *delicious*

Materials List

- 1/2 cup margarine (1 stick)
- 16 ounces marshmallows (1 pound)
- 9 cups crisp rice cereal (Generic cereal works very well.)
- A paper plate for each child
- Cinnamon redhots (Optional)
- A large bowl and a wooden spoon

1-14 Crispy Rice Snowballs

Directions

Melt the margarine and marshmallows in the top of a double boiler. Remove from the heat. [Microwave Directions: Combine the margarine and marshmallows in a microwave bowl. Cover with plastic wrap. Microwave on *high* for 3 minutes. Remove from the oven.]

Stir with a wooden spoon until smooth. Do this step on a table where the children can see. Show them how *sticky* the mixture is.

Help the children add *9* cups of crisp rice cereal. Count out loud with the children as they add the cups of cereal, "One . . . two . . . three . . . four . . . five . . . six . . . seven . . . eight . . . nine. How many cups of cereal did we add? *Nine*."

The children can take turns stirring this mixture with a wooden spoon. Have them do it one at a time, though, or you will have cereal all over the kitchen.

Print each child's name on his or her paper plate, using uppercase and lower-case letters.

Spoon a large portion onto each child's plate. Give everyone 1/2 teaspoon of margarine to rub on the palms of their hands.

Tell the children to shape their portion into a snowball, pressing it *firmly* together. Refrigerate the snowballs on the plates until they become firm, about 30 minutes. The children can make faces on their snowballs with cinnamon redhots before they are refrigerated, if you wish.

Help the children pick out their own snowball by reading the name on the plate. Note how *delicious* the snowballs taste by asking, "Aren't these *delicious* and *crisp*?"

PEANUT BUTTER/APPLE SLICES

A good time to teach children small tidbits of information is when they're sitting at the table eating tidbits of food. They will certainly be a captive audience. With this snack they will learn about apples and pairs (FIG. 1-15).

Skills to Teach

Teach children 2 years old and up:

- The meaning of *a pair*
- How many make *2*
- How to spread with a knife
- How to read his or her name

Materials List

- Paper plates
- 1 apple for each child
- Peanut butter
- A table knife or a plastic picnic knife for each child

Directions

1-15 Peanut Butter/Apple Slices

Print each child's name, using uppercase and lowercase letters, on his paper plate.

Slice and core an apple for each child. Peel them if needed. I know the peeling is good for you, but my children spit it out, and I would rather peel the apples than clean up spit-out peelings.

Give each child as many apple slices as you think he will eat and a lump of peanut butter on a paper plate.

Tell the children to spread peanut butter on one apple slice, stick on another apple slice, and eat the whole thing. Say to them, "We use *2* apple slices to make each snack. We use *a pair* of apple slices for each snack. How many make a *pair*? *Two*!"

As soon as they understand that, let them spread and eat in peace.

February

Do your children know who chopped his father's cherry tree? Do they know why Lincoln Logs have that name? February offers a chance to teach a few facts about American History, and Valentine's Day is a wonderful way to brighten up a cold, dark winter month.

Craft-Training Skills to Learn

Trying a new craft is like trying a new recipe. Just assemble the ingredients, put your imagination into gear, and follow the directions. Add a touch of this or that as you wish, to make the finished product your very own.

Use February crafts to teach the following skills:

- Learning the names of colors
- How to glue
- How to print his name
- How to draw a face
- Learning the basic geometric shapes
- Counting
- Learning *how many* make 2, 3, and 4
- How to cut, sew, and string a necklace, which teach eye-hand coordination and small motor skills.
- Learning to use descriptive words
- Learning the meaning of *large* and *small*, *top* and *bottom*, *between*, and *cooperation*.
- Learning to sit still, listen, and follow directions with cooking crafts.

Children Learn as They Cook

A child needs to know what goes into a recipe, just as he needs to know that green beans and milk come from a farm and not just a grocery store.

I know a man who loved to eat pudding until he discovered that it was made with eggs and milk. Now he hates it. I taught a class of first graders who wouldn't taste the cookie dough I brought them because they thought it was clay. "Oh no," they all said in unison, "We're not gonna taste that stuff! You can't trick us!" Only Wanda Jean would taste the dough because her mother baked cookies, and she knew what it was. I know another man who recently found out that pickles are made from cucumbers, raisins come from dried grapes, and prunes are dried-up plums.

Cook with your children. It teaches them a lot of things.

PRETZEL LOG CABIN

Abraham Lincoln was born February 12, 1809, in Hodgenville, Kentucky. His birthplace was a small 16-×-18-foot log cabin with one window and a dirt floor. He was the sixteenth president of the United States.

To understand how a log cabin looked nearly 200 years ago, you can help the children build one from Lincoln Logs, or the children can make a much cheaper model from fat pretzel sticks (FIG. 2-1). I prefer the pretzel stick log cabin because after the house-raising the children can pretend to be termites and eat the house.

Two hundred years ago, it was necessary for people to cooperate with one another, working together to build houses and barns. Since the main tools available were hatchets, saws, and hammers, everyone had to pitch in and help neighbors build the log cabin structures that made up the pioneer farm. The children's pretzel log cabin teaches them about cooperation as they take turns helping with the house-raising.

Skills to Teach

Teach children 2 years old and up:

- The *square* shape
- The colors *brown* and *green*
- The meaning of *cooperate*

Teach children 3 years old and up:

- Some historic facts about our country
- To use descriptive words such as *salty*, *crisp*, and *crunchy*

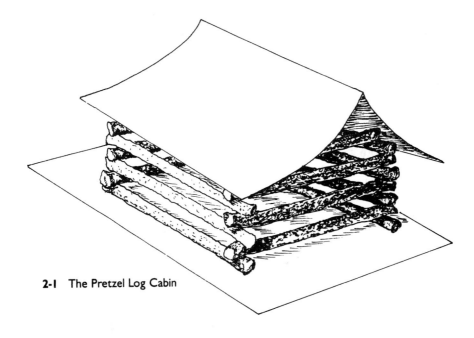

2-1 The Pretzel Log Cabin

Materials List

- A 9-ounce bag of pretzel rods. (Fat pretzels about 7 inches long, found in the snack section of supermarkets.)
- A sheet of green construction paper
- A sheet of brown construction paper

Directions

Tell the children who Abraham Lincoln was, and why we celebrate his birthday. Visit the public library and look for books on our American ancestors, the pioneers. Talk about the log cabins that were the houses for many pioneers.

Tell them, "We're going to make a *square* log cabin, and we will use pretzels instead of logs. We need to *cooperate* and work together to build our square log cabin, just as the pioneers did."

Divide the pretzels as evenly as possible among the children. Lay the sheet of green construction paper on the table. Tell the children that the *green* paper can be the *green* grass where they will build their cabin.

Help the children work together, laying the pretzels in a crisscross fashion to form a square cabin. Point out that the cabin is a *square* since each side is the same length. Help the children understand the idea of *cooperation*—that they are building the cabin by taking turns and working together.

When the cabin is complete, say to the children, "Now I will fold this sheet of *brown* paper in half to make a roof for the cabin." Lay the roof carefully atop of the cabin.

Before the children dismantle their creation for snack time, talk about it a little more. Note the spaces, or *chinks*, between the logs and ask the children if they know how President Lincoln's family kept the cold wind out of their house. (They filled the chinks with clay from a river bank, mixed with straw or dried grass. They also covered their windows with oiled paper that let the light in, and used shutters when they wanted to close the windows tightly.)

As the children eat their pretzels, ask them to think of words that describe the pretzels. Print the words in large letters on a sheet of paper as they say them, then read the words back to the children. Some descriptive words you can encourage them to use are *salty, hard, crunchy, crisp,* and *crumbly*. Tape their list of descriptive words down low where they can look at it whenever they want.

Abraham Lincoln read books by candlelight and firelight in the evenings. Try reading a story to the children by candlelight. Stick a short candle inside a tall glass to make it safer.

woolie-pullie

> When children are small, the *process* of creating is more important to them than the *product*. That is why they will work on something for a long time, and when it is finished will show very little interest in it!

TRAY EMBROIDERY

Tray Embroidery is a *process* craft that children can do as long as they want. It's easy to do when the child uses a styrofoam meat tray, a large plastic needle, and yarn. Older children can create lovely and interesting designs using many different colors of yarn. Younger children will sew just for the sake of sewing (FIG. 2-2).

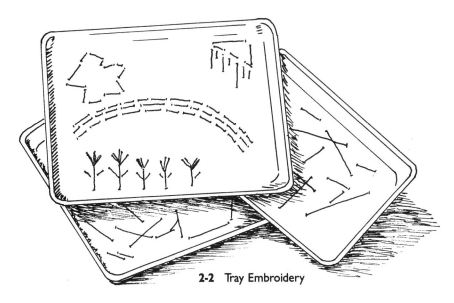

2-2 Tray Embroidery

Skills to Teach

Teach children 2 years old and up how to sew. This is a very good activity to increase eye-hand coordination and small motor skills.

Materials List

- Styrofoam meat trays
- Yarn 18 inches long
- Large plastic needles. (Look in the sewing and knitting notions section of your supermarket.)

Directions

Wash and dry the meat trays.

Tie the yard onto each needle, and tie a big knot at the other end of the yarn.

Show the children how to sew by poking the needle through a tray and turning the tray over and back. Don't expect them to do a perfect job, however. Let them do their own creating with this craft.

When they have finished sewing with the first piece of yarn, untie the needle, tie another piece of yarn to the first piece, and tie the needle on again. They can continue sewing for a long time this way.

Mark and Clark are making a Popcorn Snowman with Clark's mom as their helper.

Pam Cole helps her students, Jennifer and Mary Loretta, construct hats for their Cylinder Snowmen.

Mary and Jean-Paul are proud of their homemade Heart-Shaped Pizza.

The children punch plenty of holes while making the Paper Punch Valentine.

Aaron likes the Pinecone Owl that his dad helped him make.

Ashley, Amy, and Albert have finished their beautiful Cylinder Soldiers.

Elizabeth is helping Carrie glue her Kitchen Collage, while Jenny selects seeds and spices.

The Paper Plate Fish is bright and pretty. Its plastic lid eyes make it bob up and down.

The children gather around Peanut, the Primrose School mascot,
to show off their Paper Strip Nosegays.

Clyde the Cat and Charlie Chicken are good friends, thanks to puppeteers Albert and Jean-Paul.

Diane and Jennifer are practicing drawing skills while making the Balloon Man.

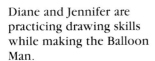

The Reindeer Goody Bag holds lots of surprises!

The Pinecone Turkey is easy to make with adult help.

Jean-Paul and his sister, Christina, count the days until Christmas with the Santa Calendar.

POM-POM CRITTER REFRIGERATOR MAGNET

The Pom-Pom Critter Magnet is a good *product* craft since the process of making it takes only a few minutes, and the child has a nice product to show off, play with, and keep. It's an excellent craft for little ones with short attention spans (FIG. 2-3)

Skills to Teach

Teach children 2 years old and up:

- The colors *red* and *white*
- Gluing skills

Teach children 4 years old and up cutting skills.

Materials List

The first three items must be purchased in a craft store. Just ask for them by name.

- 1¹/₂-inch white pom-poms
- Movable paste-on eyes, size 10 MM, two for each child
- ¹/₂-inch-wide flexible strip magnet, cut into 1-inch pieces
- Red construction paper

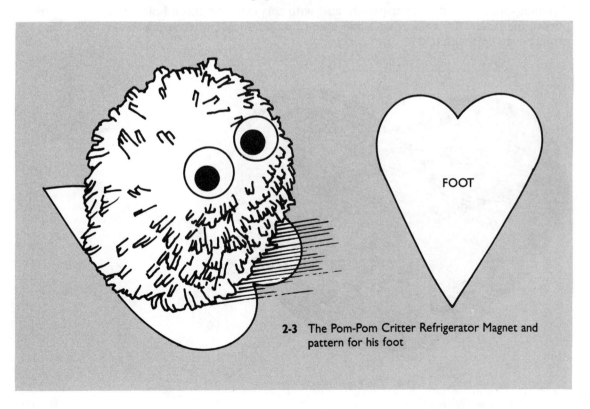

2-3 The Pom-Pom Critter Refrigerator Magnet and pattern for his foot

Directions

Use the pattern in FIG. 2-3 to trace a valentine foot onto red paper. Cut out one foot for each Critter. Children 4 years old and up should be encouraged to cut their own.

Give each child a pom-pom, two eyes, and a valentine foot. Tell them to put a small amount of glue in the middle of the *red* valentine, place the *white* pom-pom on the glue, and press down with their hand to stick the two together.

The children can glue on the eyes. Then they can add a 1-inch piece of magnet to the bottom of the Critter. The magnet comes with its own sticky backing and needs no glue.

After the Pom-Pom Critters dry, they can be used to decorate the refrigerator or to hold up notes or drawings.

woolie-pullie

When working with a group of children, put each child's craft pieces in an inexpensive plastic sandwich bag before the craft activity begins. This makes it easy and quick to pass out individual "Craft Kits." It also makes it easier for the child to keep track of numerous small shapes.

PAPER PUNCH VALENTINE

Children love to use the paper punch, and with this craft the more holes they punch, the better! Try to borrow a two-hole or a three-hole punch to make the project even more fun (FIG. 2-4).

2-4 The Paper Punch Valentine

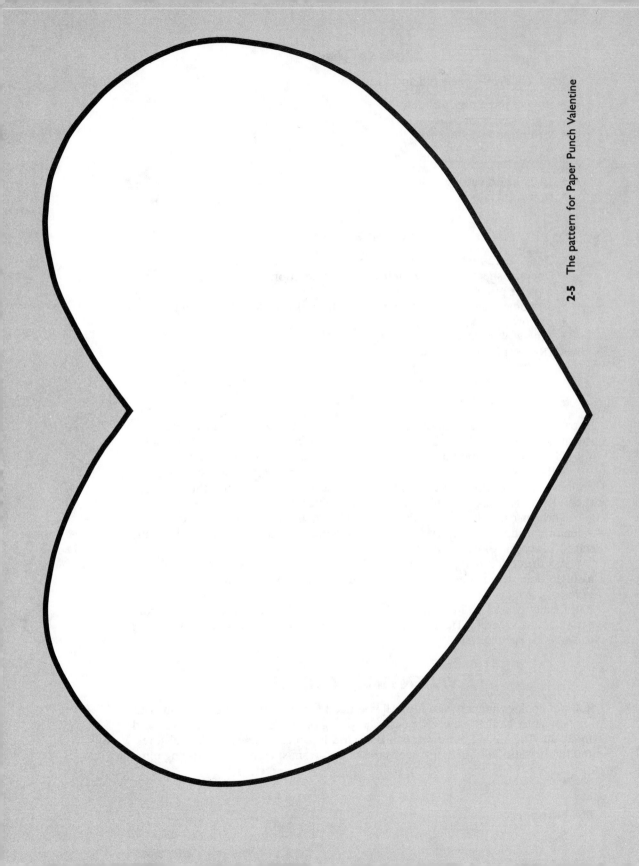

2-5 The pattern for Paper Punch Valentine

Skills to Teach

Teach children 4 years old and up:

- How to use a paper punch
- The meaning of *between*
- Writing and spelling skills

Teach children 5 years old and up:

- Tracing and cutting skills
- How to tie a bow

Materials List

- One 9-×-12-inch sheet of red or pink construction paper
- One-half sheet of 9-×-12-inch white construction paper
- A paper punch
- A two-hole and three-hole paper punch (optional)
- Narrow-tipped red marker
- Notebook reinforcers
- 18-inch piece of narrow ribbon

Directions

Instruct the children as follows: "Use the pattern in FIG. 2-5 on p. 27 to trace one valentine on white paper and two valentines on red or pink paper. Cut them out." You will need to do the tracing and cutting for children younger than five.

Tell the children to use the paper punch to punch holes all over both *red* valentines. To make holes in the middle, fold the valentines, punch them, unfold them. Fold them again a different way and punch some more.

Then instruct them to write a message such as "I Love You" on the white valentine, using narrow-tipped red markers. Have the children sign the valentine with "Love, (his or her name)."

Ask the children to put the white valentine *between* the two red ones. Punch a single hole through all three, near the top. Put a notebook reinforcer on the holes.

Finally, put an 18-inch narrow ribbon through the reinforced holes to hold the valentine together. Tie it in a pretty bow. Now ask them to give the valentine to someone special.

VALENTINE COOKIES

Roll-out cookies are easy and fun. All you need is a smooth plastic cloth on your kitchen table, a valentine cookie cutter, a rolling pin with a stockinette cover, and an apron. The rolling pin cover can be found in supermarkets, hardware stores, and kitchen specialty shops; it keeps the dough from sticking to the rolling pin.

Skills to Teach

Teach children 2 years old and up:

- How to roll and cut cookie dough, which is much like clay
- To sit still, listen, and follow directions
- How to print his or her name

Materials List

- A large bowl
- A wooden spoon or an electric mixer
- 3/4 cup shortening
- 1 cup sugar
- Two eggs
- 1/2 teaspoon vanilla
- 2 1/2 cups flour
- 1 teaspoon baking powder
- 1 teaspoon salt
- Extra flour
- Valentine cookie cutter
- A rolling pin with a stockinette cover
- Paper plates

Directions

Pull up each child's sleeves and let them kneel on chairs. Tie an apron on each child, as high up as it will go to cover as much of their shirts as possible.

Measure the shortening, sugar, eggs, and vanilla into the large bowl. Let the children help with the measuring. Use an electric mixer to blend the ingredients thoroughly, or let the children mix them with a wooden spoon. Wooden spoons are nice to use because the shortening and eggs don't slide past them, and they are not noisy.

Measure the flour, baking powder, and salt. Let the children add them to the cookie mixture. After the children have mixed the dough thoroughly, cover it, and refrigerate it for an hour or longer.

A smooth plastic cloth on your kitchen table makes a good place to roll out the dough. Put a small pile of flour in front of each aproned child, and let him smooth it around on the tabletop. Give him a portion of dough.

Help the children roll their dough 1/4 inch thick. Show them how to use the cookie cutter to cut the dough. Use a wide spatula to transfer the cookies to an ungreased baking sheet.

Sprinkle them with red sugar, if desired. To make your own red sugar, put a cup of granulated sugar in a plastic bag. Add a drop or two of red food coloring, close the bag tightly, and shake hard.

Bake in a preheated oven at 400°F for 6 to 8 minutes, or until the cookies are lightly browned around the edges.

While waiting for the cookies to bake, give everyone a paper plate and a pencil. Ask each child to print his or her name on a plate so each person can have his own cookies to eat and share.

When the cookies are done, pop them onto the children's plates to cool.

HEART-SHAPED PIZZA

Another Valentine's treat that you can serve for lunch or a snack is a heart-shaped pizza (FIG. 2-6).

2-6 The Heart-Shaped Pizza

Skills to Teach

Teach children 2 years old and up:

- To sit still, listen, and follow directions
- How to grease a pan and spread dough
- How to measure, stir, and bake

Teach children 6 years old and up how to shred cheese.

Materials List

- A large jelly roll pan
- A large bowl and a wooden spoon

- 1 cup warm water
- 1/2 cup powdered milk
- 1 package active dry yeast
- 1 tablespoon sugar
- 1 1/2 teaspoons salt
- 2 1/2 cups flour
- 1/2 pound (8 oz.) mozzarella cheese
- 1 pound ground beef
- 1 cup tomato sauce, spaghetti sauce, or pizza sauce
- 1/2 teaspoon oregano

Directions

Show the children how to grease the jelly roll pan by spreading shortening on it with their hands. They can write letters and numbers on the greased pan with their fingers if they are not in a hurry to eat.

Help the children measure the warm water, powdered milk, yeast, sugar, and salt into the bowl. Let the children take turns stirring the mixture with the wooden spoon.

Help the children add 2 1/2 cups of flour. Let them stir it vigorously until the dough is smooth and falls away from the spoon in sheets. Add more flour until the dough loses its stickiness. Turn it onto the greased pan.

Let the dough sit for 10 minutes so it can rise slightly. Oil the children's hands and let them push and spread the dough into as large a valentine shape as possible. Pinch up the edges to hold the pizza filling.

Pour the tomato sauce on the dough. Let the children spread it to the edges of the dough with their fingers.

Crumble and fry the ground beef until it loses its redness. Drain off the fat. Spoon the meat on top of the tomato sauce. Sprinkle with oregano.

Bake in a preheated oven at 425 °F for 20 minutes, or until the crust is brown and the pizza is bubbly.

While the pizza is baking, shred the cheese. Children 6 years old and up can do the shredding, but younger children will shred their fingers along with the cheese.

After the pizza is browned, remove it from the oven and sprinkle it evenly with the cheese. Return it to the oven until the cheese melts. Heart-shaped pizza tastes good cold as well as hot.

GIANT FAMILY VALENTINE

Hang the Giant Family Valentine with a red ribbon or yarn to surprise a special person, whether it be a teacher, a principal, or a mommy and daddy.

Skills to Teach

Teach children 2 years old and up:

- The colors *red* and *white*
- The meaning of *large* and *small*

- Drawing and gluing skills
- How to write his or her name

Teach children 4 years old and up:

- Cutting skills
- How to create something nice for someone else

Materials List

- White poster board. (Look in the school supplies section of your drugstore.)
- Red poster board
- Scissors
- Glue
- Water-based markers
- Red ribbon or yarn

Directions

The children and you should decide who will receive the Giant Valentine. Leave the white poster board flat to form the card. Cut the red poster board into a giant valentine. Use the red scraps to draw small valentines.

Children 4 years old and up can cut out these *small red* valentines and glue them onto the *large white* poster board. You must do the cutting for younger children.

Let each child draw on the Giant Valentine, write messages on it, and sign his or her name.

Punch or cut a hole in each top corner. Tie on the red ribbon or yarn to hang it, or tape it to the wall or door.

woolie-pullie

Along the same lines as the Giant Family Valentine is the Welcome Home Sign which can be made from any large piece of plain paper—the larger the better. Whenever a family member is away from home for a night or two, a Welcome Home Sign and maybe a cake or cupcakes can become a nice tradition. It makes that person feel very special.

In our family we make a sign when Daddy goes on business trips, when a child goes to camp or visits a relative for a week or so, or when someone returns from a hospital stay. Sometimes the children add a favorite magazine cutout to the sign, sometimes they draw pictures on it, and sometimes they write happy messages, depending on their ages. Then they tape it to the front door or to the wall just inside the door. If we bake a cake, we leave it on the kitchen table and have a party when our special person comes home.

VALENTINE BAG

Valentine Bags are great to use to carry the valentines the children have made for friends, to carry pastel candy hearts from the store, or to carry cookies they have baked (FIG. 2-7).

Skills to Teach

Teach children 2 years old and up:

- The colors *red*, *white*, and *pink*
- The meaning of *top* and *bottom*
- Gluing skills

Teach children 4 years old and up cutting skills

Materials List

- White pastry bags from a supermarket bakery shop. (Brown sandwich bags will do if you can't get the white ones.)
- Red, white, and pink construction paper
- Water-based markers or crayons
- Pencils
- Scissors
- Glue

2-7 A Valentine Bag

Directions

Before beginning this craft, cut out lots of small valentine hearts from the red, white, and pink construction paper. For children 4 years old and up, trace or draw valentines on the construction paper for them to cut out.

Say to the children, "Here is a *white* bag and a pencil for each of you. Please write your name on the *bottom* of the bag so we will know it's yours." Help each child print his or her name on the bottom of the bag, using uppercase and lowercase letters.

Now tell the children, "Open your bag at the *top*. You can decorate it by gluing valentines on it and drawing on it."

VALENTINES-AND-STRAWS JEWELRY

Valentine's Day can become even more of a celebration if the children can "dress up" with special jewelry made especially for that day (FIG. 2-8).

Skills to Teach

Teach children 2 years old and up:

- The colors *red* and *white*
- How to thread small things on a needle. (This step is very good for developing eye-hand coordination and small motor skills.)

Materials List

- Red construction paper
- Skinny red-and-white-striped drinking straws
- A large plastic needle for each child
- Red or white embroidery thread or yarn
- Scissors

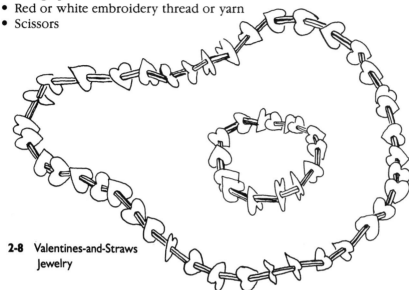

2-8 Valentines-and-Straws Jewelry

Directions

Pleat the red construction paper into folds 1/2-inch wide. Cut out many small valentines at one time.

Snip the drinking straws into 1/2-inch pieces. Hold a bunch of straws together and cut them with scissors while both hands and the straws are inside a single plastic bag to prevent the snipped pieces from flying all over the place.

Tie a 26-inch piece of yarn or embroidery thread onto a needle for each child. Tie a piece of snipped straw on the other end of the thread or yarn to keep the necklace pieces from falling off of it.

Tell the children to thread the *red* valentines by pushing the needle through the center of each one. Show them how to alternate the paper valentines with the *red-and-white-striped* straws until the thread is filled.

Remove the needle and tie the ends of the necklace together. Make a bracelet the same way, using a 12-inch piece of yarn.

The children can make two bracelets and hang them over their ears, for earrings.

PAPER HATCHET

George Washington was born February 22, 1732, at Bridges Creek, Virginia. When he was about 6 years old he received a hatchet with which he chopped and killed one of his father's prize cherry trees. His father asked who had killed the tree, and in the story that has become legend, young George stepped forward to take his punishment. "Father," he said, "I cannot tell a lie. I chopped the cherry tree."

He did not say, "I chopped *down* the cherry tree." Actually, he chopped the bark off, and it took awhile for the tree to die. This small incident in history gives us ample excuse to lecture children on the virtues of being honest, since George Washington grew up to be our first president and the father of our country.

With a Paper Hatchet, the children can practice "chopping" without destroying anything (FIG. 2-9).

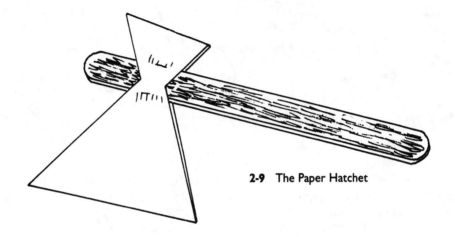

2-9 The Paper Hatchet

Skills to Teach

Teach children 2 years old and up:

- The colors *yellow* and *brown*
- The meaning of *between*
- How many make *2*
- Some facts on American History
- Gluing skills
- How to write his or her name

Teach children 4 years old and up cutting skills.

Materials List

- A popsicle stick for each hatchet
- A ballpoint pen
- Yellow construction paper
- A brown water-based marker
- Scissors
- Glue

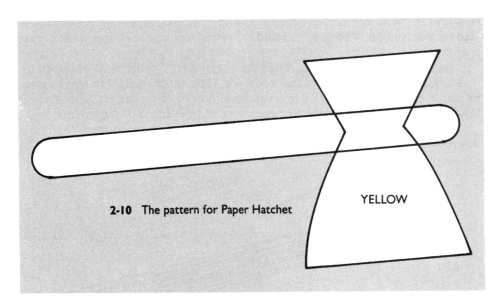

2-10 The pattern for Paper Hatchet

YELLOW

Directions

Use the pattern in FIG. 2-10 to trace two hatchet blades on yellow construction paper for each child. Cut them out for younger children, but encourage children 4 years old and up to do their own cutting.

Give each child a popsicle stick with instructions to write his or her name on it with the ballpoint pen, pressing down hard.

Tell the children to color the popsicle stick *brown* with the *brown* water-based marker. They will be able to read the name through the brown stain. Water-based markers, incidentally, are nice to use with children because the bright colors wash off hands, faces, clothes, and plastic tablecloths.

Give two hatchet blades to each child. Tell them the story of George Washington and his father's cherry tree. Then add, "To make a toy hatchet like George Washington's real one, glue the two *yellow* hatchet blades together with the popsicle stick *between* them.

Let the hatchets dry before the children practice chopping with them.

woolie-pullie

Put white glue in catsup or mustard squirt bottles. Use these bottles to fill individual milk lids at craft time. The squirt bottles are fast to use and easy to unplug.

PAPER CHERRIES

Paper cherries can be pinned to a child's shirt or taped to a door or wall in honor of Washington's birthday (FIG. 2-11).

Skills to Teach

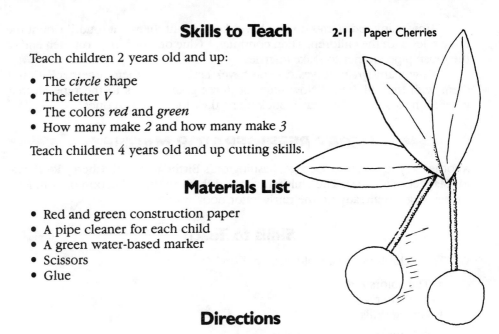

Teach children 2 years old and up:

- The *circle* shape
- The letter *V*
- The colors *red* and *green*
- How many make *2* and how many make *3*

Teach children 4 years old and up cutting skills.

Materials List

- Red and green construction paper
- A pipe cleaner for each child
- A green water-based marker
- Scissors
- Glue

Directions

Use the pattern in FIG. 2-12 to draw two circles on red construction paper and three leaves on green construction paper for each child. Cut them out for the younger children, but encourage those 4 years old and up to cut their own.

Give each child a pipe cleaner, two circle cherries, and three leaves. The children should color their pipe cleaners *green* with the water-based marker.

Tell the children the following: "Bend your *green* pipe cleaner in half to make the letter *V*.

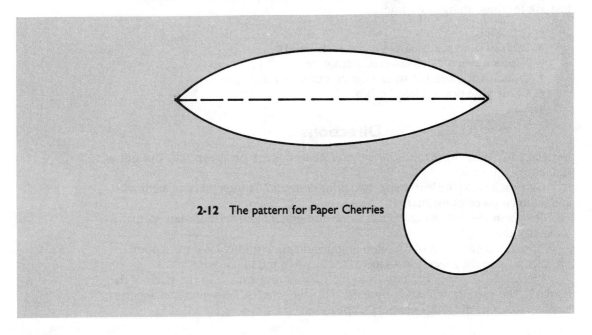

2-12 The pattern for Paper Cherries

"How many *red circles* do you have? Let's count them out loud." Count the red circles with the children. Then continue, "Glue one *red circle* on each end of the *green* pipe cleaner to make cherries.

"How many *green* leaves do you have? Let's count them together." Count them with the children. "Now glue the *three green* leaves to the pipe cleaner where it bends. Make the leaves stick up so they look like real ones."

CHERRY REFRIGERATOR MAGNET

Another way to celebrate George Washington's Birthday is with Cherry Refrigerator Magnets (FIG. 2-13). The children can add them to the collection of Pom-Pom Critter Magnets already on the refrigerator door.

Skills to Teach

Teach children 2 years old and up:

- The colors *red* and *green*
- The letter *V*
- Gluing skills

Teach children 4 years old and up:

- To follow directions
- To create a useful craft in honor of Washington's birthday

Materials List

Except for the glue, everything for this craft must be purchased in a craft store. Just ask for these things by name:

- Green felt
- Two red pom-poms, size $5/8$, for each child
- $2^1/4$-inch green cloth-covered stem wire
- $1/2$-inch-wide flexible strip magnet, cut into 1-inch pieces
- A little glue poured into jar lids

Directions

Use the pattern in FIG. 2-13 to trace the three-leaf shape on green felt. Cut out a shape for each child.

Give each child the leaf shape, two pom-poms, a $2^1/4$-inch piece of stem wire, and a 1-inch piece of magnet.

Tell them the following: "First, bend the *green* stem wire in half so that it looks like the letter *V*.

"Next, dip each end of the wire in glue and stick it into a *red* pom-pom.

"Now glue the *green* leaf shape to the bend in the *green* wire.

"Remove the paper backing from the magnet and stick it to the back of the leaves." The magnet will stick by itself. Use the Cherry Refrigerator Magnet to hold up notes or drawings on metal appliances.

2-13 The Cherry Refrigerator Magnet
and pattern

Leaf

March

The windy month of March makes us think of kites and approaching spring. The children can make kites and fly them on the coat closet door. They can make Pinwheel Flowers before the first crocus blooms. Spring can arrive indoors even if it doesn't outdoors.

March Marches into the House

Personally, March reminds me of mud. Maybe that's because I have four children, a cat, and a dog, and that's what they track in all month.

Fighting March mud is a constant battle. I tried putting newspapers by the front door for the children's boots, and they thought they were supposed to lie on the floor and read. The dog thought he was being paper-trained again.

We lived in a house in Illinois that had red carpeting and the mud was black. Then we moved to a house in Georgia that had black carpeting; the mud there is red. March crafts kept the children indoors and out of the mud.

Craft-Training Skills to Learn

With this month's projects, the children again encounter plenty of colors, shapes, and cooking crafts. One craft, the Butterfly, is especially for older children; another project, the Pot of Flowers, will help younger children learn to cut with scissors.

Use March crafts to teach the following skills:

- Learning the names of colors
- Learning the basic geometric shapes
- How to cut, glue, color, paint, tie, and use tape
- How to print his or her name
- Learning the meaning of *on top of*
- How to use lacing cards, another good coordination exercise
- How to put things together, also called assembling skills
- How to create with dough, which is just like clay
- For older children, using a ruler to draw and measure
- Learning the meaning of *first* through *sixth*

HANG-UP KITE

Bring spring into the house with brightly colored Hang-Up Kites (FIG. 3-1).

Skills to Teach

Teach children 2 years old and up:

- The colors *red, yellow, blue, pink, black,* and *green*
- The *diamond, circle,* and *triangle* shapes
- The meaning of *on top of*
- Gluing skills

Teach children 4 years old and up:

- Cutting skills
- How to tie. (Sometimes 3-year-olds can tie, too.)
- The meaning of *first* through *sixth*

Materials List

- A large piece of paper for each kite. (Grocery bags work well, or use computer or construction paper.)
- Red, yellow, blue, pink, black, and green construction paper
- Red yarn 24 inches long
- 4 pieces of ribbon or cloth for each kite, cut into 1¹/₂-×-6-inch strips.
- Scissors
- Glue

3-1 The Hang-Up Kite

Directions

For each kite, open the side and bottom seams of a large paper grocery bag (if that is what you decide to use) so that it will lay flat. Using a ruler, draw a diamond shape on the bag, making each side of the diamond 12 inches long.

Cut the diamond out for younger children. Encourage children 4 years old and up to cut their own diamond.

Using the patterns in FIGS. 3-2 and 3-3, trace the following on construction paper: two blue eyes, two black eyeballs, two pink cheeks, two yellow hairs, a green nose, and a red mouth. Again, cut these shapes out for younger children, but encourage older children to cut their own.

Say the following to the children, "Your kite is shaped like a *diamond*. What shape is it? A *diamond*!

"*First*, glue the *blue circle* eyes on the *diamond*.

"*Second*, glue the *black circle* eyeballs *on top of* the *blue circle* eyes.

"*Third*, glue the *red* mouth on your *diamond*." Help everyone glue these pieces in their proper places.

"*Fourth*, glue the *green triangle* nose on the *diamond* kite.

"*Fifth*, glue the *yellow* hair on the *diamond*.
"*Sixth*, glue on the *pink circle* cheeks."
Make a small hole in the bottom corner of each kite. Each child can tie his or her piece of *red* yarn through this hole. Then he can tie the four strips of cloth at intervals along the yarn to create a kite tail.

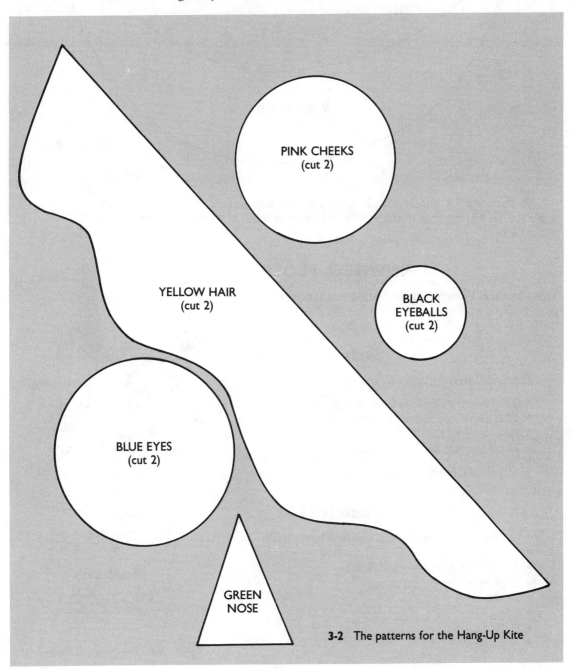

3-2 The patterns for the Hang-Up Kite

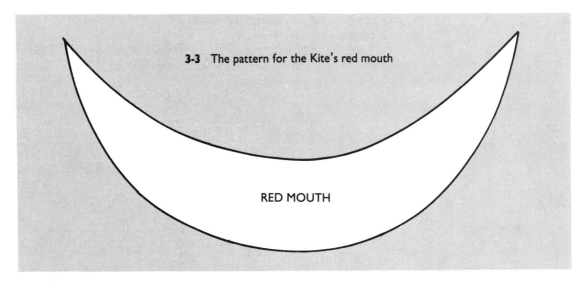

3-3 The pattern for the Kite's red mouth

RED MOUTH

To decorate for windy March days, tape the kite onto a door or wall at an angle so that it appears as though the wind were blowing it, with the tail streaming along behind.

PINWHEEL FLOWER

This Pinwheel Flower will also bring a burst of spring into your home (FIG. 3-4).

Skills to Teach

Teach children 2 years old and up:

- The colors *yellow*, *brown*, and *green*
- The *circle* and *square* shapes
- How to use tape
- How to write his or her name

Teach children 4 years old and up cutting skills.

Materials List

- Yellow, brown and green construction paper
- Crayons
- A popsicle stick for each flower
- A green water-based marker
- Pencil
- Scissors
- Cellophane tape
- A stapler

3-4 The Pinwheel Flower

Directions

For each flower, use the pattern in FIG. 3-5 to draw a 6-inch square on yellow construction paper. Trace the dotted lines and the five dots onto the square. Trace the flowerpot onto brown construction paper and the small circle onto green paper (FIG. 3-6). Cut these parts out for children younger than 4 years. Encourage children 4 years old and up to cut their own.

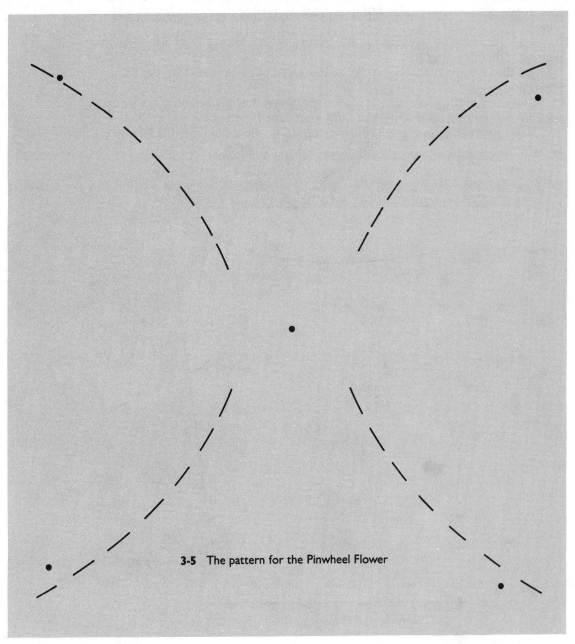

3-5 The pattern for the Pinwheel Flower

Give each child a square, a flowerpot, a circle, and a popsicle stick.

Tell them to decorate the *yellow square* on both sides with bright crayon drawings. Tell them to color the popsicle stick all over with the *green* marker.

Tell each child to print his or her name on the front of the *brown* flowerpot, as neatly as possible. Make sure he holds his pencil correctly and uses uppercase and lowercase letters. Then he can decorate his flowerpot.

Cut the square on the dotted lines. Older children can cut their own. Curl the four *dotted* corners to the center of the square and staple in place, forming a pinwheel.

Next, staple the pinwheel to the end of the popsicle stick. Cut a 1/2-inch slit in the top of the flowerpot.

Tell the children to insert the end of the *green* popsicle stick into the *brown* flowerpot.

Give each child a piece of cellophane tape. Show the children how to tape the stick in place on the back of the pot. Add more tape if necessary.

Now they can glue the *small green circle* in the center of the Pinwheel Flower.

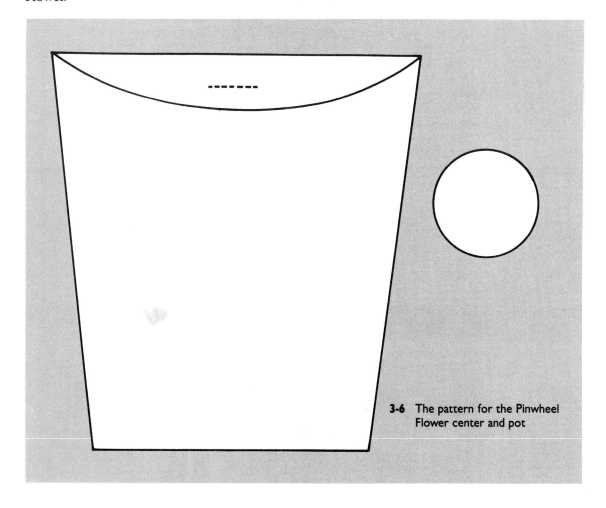

3-6 The pattern for the Pinwheel Flower center and pot

BUTTERFLY

This rather complicated craft will challenge older children. When finished, they will have a beautiful butterfly that softly flaps its wings as they move the midsection up and down (FIG. 3-7).

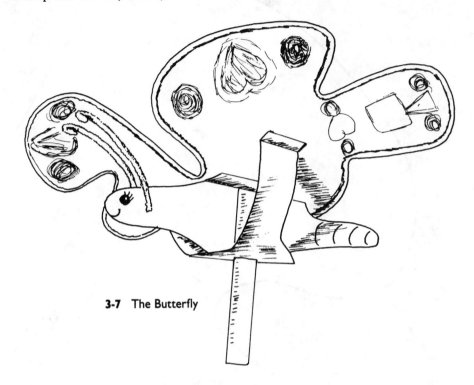

3-7 The Butterfly

Skills to Teach

Teach children 4 years old and up cutting, gluing, and assembling skills.

Materials List

- Pastel construction paper or lightweight cardboard
- Crayons
- Scissors
- Glue
- Glitter

Directions

For each butterfly trace the four pattern pieces onto construction paper or cardboard (FIGS. 3-8 and 3-9). Let the children cut them out and decorate them with bright crayon drawings before putting them together.

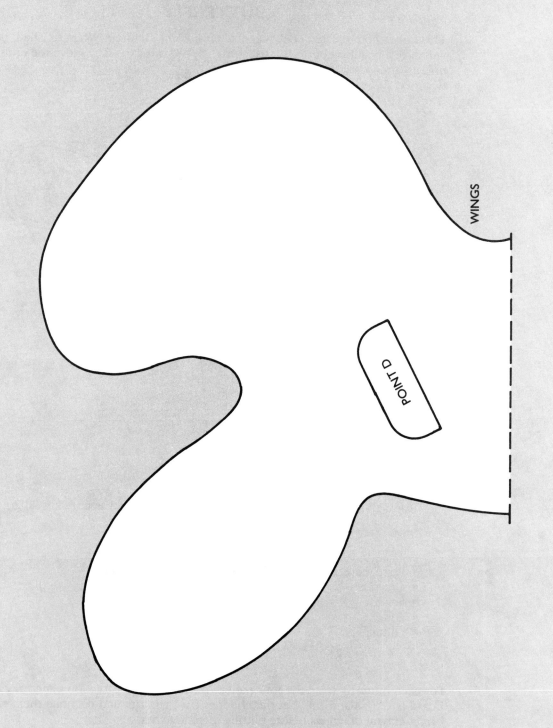

WIINGS

POINT D

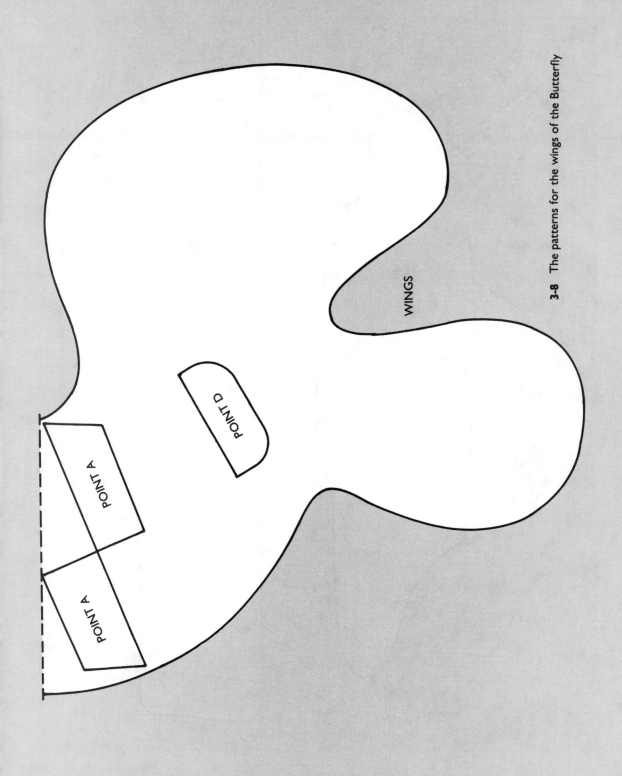

WINGS

POINT A

POINT A

POINT D

3-8 The patterns for the wings of the Butterfly

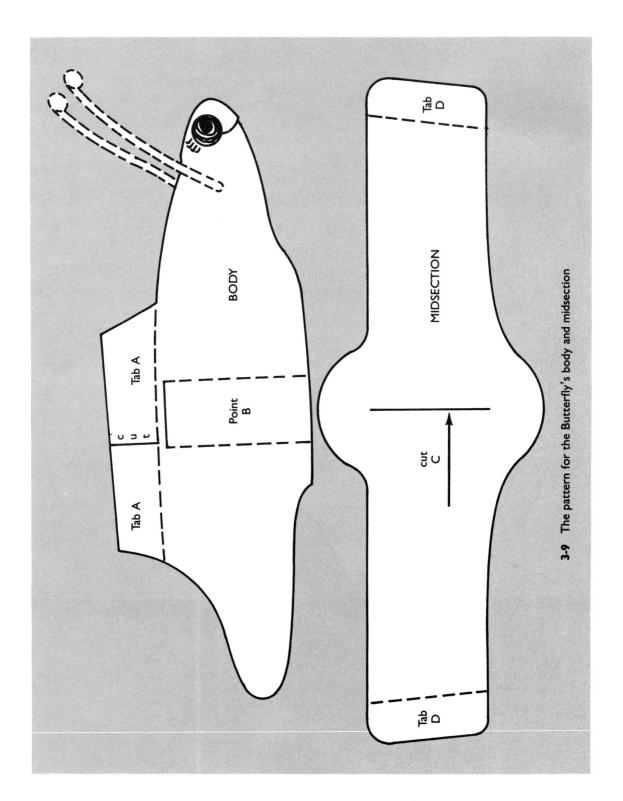

3-9 The pattern for the Butterfly's body and midsection

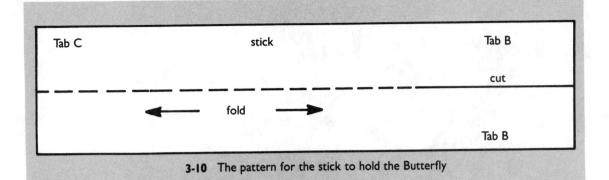

3-10 The pattern for the stick to hold the Butterfly

The children should fasten the body to the underside of the wings by putting glue on TABS *A* of the body (FIG. 3-9), and centering the body on the wings at POINT *A* (FIG. 3-8).

Help the children fold the stick down the middle as indicated in FIG. 3-10.

Insert the body in the stick at the cut. Help the children glue TABS *B* of the stick onto the body at POINT *B*. Glue the stick shut the rest of the way down its length to make a handle.

Insert TAB *C* into CUT *C* in the midsection. Push the midsection up to the Butterfly's body as far as it will go.

The children should glue TABS *D* of the midsection to the underside of the wings at POINTS *D*. Lay the Butterfly upside down to dry.

When the glue is completely dry, the children can squirt glue on the top of the wings. Hold the Butterfly over a newspaper or paper towel, and pour glitter on the glue. Shake off the excess and return it to the glitter container.

Make the Butterfly "fly" by holding the stick in one hand and gently moving the midsection up and down with the other hand. Add skinny paper antennae, or tape one-half of the pipe cleaner to each side of the head.

POT OF FLOWERS

This project is designed to help younger children, as well as older children, learn to cut with scissors (FIG. 3-11).

Skills to Teach

Teach children 2 years old and up:

- Cutting skills
- Gluing skills
- The meaning of *on top of*
- The *circle* shape
- Coloring skills

Teach children 4 years old and up cutting and assembling skills.

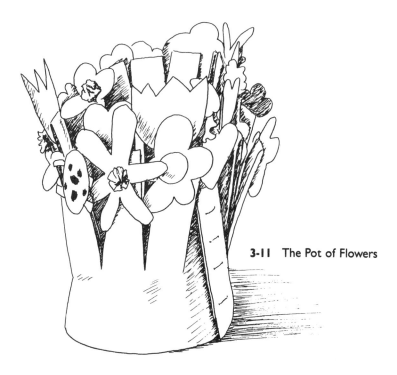

3-11 The Pot of Flowers

Materials List

- Construction paper, different colors
- A ruler and pencil
- A stapler
- A seed catalogue or magazine with flower pictures
- Scissors
- Glue
- Tissue wrapping paper (optional)

Directions

Tell your children to fold two sheets of construction paper in half lengthwise. Using the ruler and pencil, draw 3-inch-long lines from the folded side of the paper toward the open side. Draw 10 lines at 1-inch intervals. Cut on the lines. Children 8 years old and up can use the ruler to measure and draw their own lines. Younger children cannot draw the lines, but they can cut them. Help children 2 years old and up learn to cut them with scissors.

Repeat the drawing and cutting of lines on the second sheet of folded paper. Tell the children to lay one paper *on top of* the other, with one paper raised 1 inch above the other.

Help the children hold the papers together and curl them into a *circle* with the raised paper on the inside of the *circle*. Staple the circle closed.

3-12 The patterns for the Pot of Flowers

The children can cut and glue construction paper flowers or flowers from seed catalogues on each strip of paper that sticks up. They can use their imaginations to draw and cut out hearts, ladybugs, little pieces of crumpled tissue wrapping paper, or whatever else they want. You can also use the patterns in FIG. 3-12 to trace, cut out, and color things to glue on the pot.

The result is a very colorful and attractive Pot of Flowers that stands by itself.

LACING CARDS

The Lacing Cards will help teach very young children shapes as well as eye-hand coordination (FIG. 3-13).

Skills to Teach

Teach children 2 years old and up:

- The *circle, square, rectangle, triangle,* and *diamond* shapes
- Lacing skills—a very good activity to increase eye-hand coordination and small motor skills

Materials List

- 5 or more Styrofoam meat trays
- Several permanent markers in assorted colors
- A ruler
- A sharp pencil
- 5 long shoelaces

3-13 Lacing Cards

Directions

Wash and dry the Styrofoam meat trays. They can be any shape and color.

Use permanent markers to draw one large shape on each tray. You can use a cereal bowl or coffee cup to draw a circle on the first tray. Use the ruler to draw a square, rectangle, triangle, and diamond on the other four trays.

Use the sharp pencil to poke holes at 1-inch intervals in the trays to outline the shapes.

Tie a knot in the end of each shoelace. Show the children how to lace around the outside of the shape.

Teach them the names of the shapes and their colors at the same time by saying, "Here's a lacing card with a *green circle* on it. Would you like to lace it?"

When a child has finished with one card, say. "You did such a good job lacing this *green circle*. What shape did you lace? A *circle*! That's right!" No, they will not think you're crazy. Yes, they will learn their colors and shapes.

When they lose interest in a particular tray, or when it breaks, just save the shoelace and design another one.

As your children become adept at lacing, you can create more complex and challenging cards by drawing pictures of cars, houses, butterflies, or whatever. They can even design their own cards with your help.

FLOUR-SALT DOUGH

Flour-salt dough is a lot of fun because just about anything can be created from it. The children's creations become hard when they dry; so they can be kept forever. Flour-salt dough is cheap to make, it doesn't require any special ingredients, and it cleans up easily. If anyone eats it, he or she will not make that mistake twice; so roll up their sleeves, put on painting coats, and try this project in the kitchen.

Skills to Teach

Teach children 2 years old and up:

- How to work with dough
- How to create

Materials List

- 4 cups flour
- 1 cup salt
- 1½ cups water
- A large bowl
- A baking sheet or two
- Aluminum foil to cover the baking sheet

The following things are optional, depending on what the children make from the dough:

- Food colors
- Watercolors or tempera paints with brushes

- A rolling pin and cookie cutters
- Yarn for making necklaces and mobiles
- Paper clips for tree ornaments
- A garlic press or coarse sieve to make hair or fur
- Round sticks like those used in corn dogs and taffy apples to make vehicle axles

Directions

Measure the flour, salt, and water into a large bowl. Knead by hand for a few minutes until smooth. The children will be glad to help you.

You can divide the dough into four pieces and add a few drops of red, blue, or yellow food coloring to three of them. Leave the fourth piece white. Knead in the color, then give each child a portion of dough and a small pile of flour.

The things that can be made from the dough are endless. Smaller children like to make "cookies" to feed to their stuffed animals. They make them by rolling a ball of dough and then pressing it flat on the tabletop. Bird nests with eggs are easy to make: just roll a ball of dough, make a dent in the middle to form a nest, then put several small balls in the dent to look like eggs. Roll a long coil to make a snake. They can curl a long snake around a circle of dough, building it up with more coils to make a coiled pot.

The children can use a rolling pin to roll out the dough. Then they can cut it with cookie cutters. Punch a hole in each piece before baking so the pieces can be strung with yarn to make a mobile or a necklace.

To make tree ornaments for Christmas, insert a paper clip into the top of the dough shape before it is baked. Then it can be hung after it is hard.

Older children can be quite imaginative with their creations. They can shape a Santa Claus (FIG. 3-14) and glue cotton on the finished product for a beard. To make fur from the dough, they can force it through a garlic press or a coarse sieve, lift it off with a knife, and stick it on their creation with a little water.

Making dough racing cars and trucks is a favorite with boys. First the children should shape the car or truck body and four separate wheels. Next, he should poke the wooden sticks through each wheel to make the proper hole before baking. Then he should insert the axles into the car or truck body. Bake the vehicle with the axles inserted in it. Keep the wheels separate during baking, laying them flat on the baking sheet. Put the wheels on the axles after they are dry. Your child will have a car or truck Fred Flintstone would envy.

To bake everything, cover the baking sheet with aluminum foil and put the dough shapes on it. Bake in a preheated oven at 225 °F for many hours, depending on the thickness of the clay shape. The pieces need to dry out completely without browning. It helps to turn them over halfway through the baking. You can leave them in the oven overnight if necessary; just remember to take them out before you use the oven to cook supper the next day.

3-14 A Flour-Salt Dough Santa

The dried pieces can be painted with tempera or watercolors on another day. For a really fancy look, coat with clear nail polish.

woolie-pullie

> The kitchen oven is used many times in this book. When several children are baking their own creations of flour-salt dough, cookies, Bake-A-Shape, or whatever, it's important to remember whose dough is whose creation. You can do this in two ways.
>
> First, cover the baking sheet with aluminum foil. Use a black permanent marker to write the child's initials on the foil next to his or her dough.
>
> Second, if the children are working on a project in which no foil can be used, such as most cookie recipes, use the permanent marker to write tiny initials for each child directly on the baking sheet, near the edge. Put the child's dough next to his or her initials. The writing will eventually disappear after many washings, and it will not hurt the baking sheets.

TAFFY PULL

Butter everyone's hands and get ready for an old-fashioned taffy pull!

Skills to Teach

Teach children 2 years old and up:

- To sit still, listen, and follow directions
- How to measure
- How to write his or her name
- To count to *3*

Materials List

- 1 cup sugar
- 3 tablespoons cornstarch
- 1/8 teaspoon salt
- 1/2 cup water
- 2/3 cup honey
- A large heavy pot and a wooden spoon
- Paper plates
- Crayons
- Waxed paper

Directions

Help children measure and pour the sugar, cornstarch, and salt into the large heavy pot. As they add the 3 tablespoons of cornstarch, count to *three* with them, out loud. They can take turns mixing these ingredients until they are blended.

Help the children add the water and honey. Stir to blend.

Now take over to prevent burns. Stirring occasionally, boil the candy over high heat until it forms a hard ball when a small amount is dropped into a bowl of cold water.

Pour it onto a buttered plate. When it cools enough to be handled, give each child a glob to be pulled with his buttered hands. The children can pull it into long strings, fold it together, and pull again.

When the taffy turns white and can't be pulled any more, it is ready to eat. Give everyone a paper plate and crayons. They can decorate their plates and print their names on the front. Lay a piece of waxed paper on their decorated plates to keep their candy creations from sticking.

ST. PATRICK'S DAY MILKSHAKE

This milkshake is simple to make. The children can put all the ingredients in a blender and turn it on and off. Just remember to put the lid on first.

Skills to Teach

Teach children 2 years old and up:

- How to measure and count
- How to use a blender

Materials List

- One ripe banana
- One raw egg
- 2 cups milk
- 2 tablespoons sugar
- 1/2 teaspoon vanilla
- Three drops green food coloring
- A blender

Directions

Help the children measure everything into the blender container. Count the cups of milk, the tablespoons of sugar, and the drops of food coloring out loud with the children as these things are added.

Process on "high" until smooth, which should take about 30 seconds. This recipe makes about 3 cups of milkshake, but it foams a lot so it seems like more.

CAKE MIX COOKIES

Buy the very cheapest cake mix you can find, in any flavor. Generic mixes work fine; mixes with pudding in them make delicious crisp cookies. I like to stock up on them when they are on sale.

Skills to Teach

Teach children 2 years old and up:

- To sit still, listen, and follow directions
- How to measure, stir, and bake
- How to write his or her name

Materials List

- 1 package cake mix
- 1/4 cup flour
- 1/4 cup water
- 1/2 cup oil
- 1 egg
- A large bowl and a wooden spoon
- Paper plates and crayons
- Waxed paper

Optional Ingredients:

- Coconut
- Raisins
- Nuts
- Chocolate chips
- Crushed peppermint sticks
- Food coloring
- Wheat germ
- Mashed banana

Directions

Help the children measure and pour the cake mix, flour, water, oil, and egg into the large bowl. They can take turns stirring with the wooden spoon until the dough is thoroughly blended.

Now the children can add any of the optional ingredients listed. Chocolate cake mix and nuts make a good combination, for example. For St. Patrick's Day, they can add a few drops of green food coloring and 1/4 cup coconut to a white cake mix to make green cookies.

Help the children drop the dough from a teaspoon onto an ungreased baking sheet, placing the cookies a little apart. The children can roll the dough into balls the size of a walnut, then roll each ball in granulated sugar before baking to make sugar cookies. They can roll the balls in chopped nuts, which works well with chocolate dough.

Bake in a preheated oven at 350°F for 10 minutes, or until the edges just begin to turn brown. Do not overbake.

While the cookies are baking, give each child a paper plate and crayons. Each child should decorate a "cookie plate" and write his or her name on it, using uppercase and lowercase letters. Lay waxed paper on the plates to prevent crayon from getting on hot cookies.

I don't know how many cookies this recipe makes; I've never baked a whole batch because we eat a lot of them before baking.

NO-COOK PEANUT BUTTER BALLS

An easy treat to make, Peanut Butter Balls use no energy except the children's.

Skills to Teach

- To sit still, listen, and follow directions
- How to write his or her name
- How to work with dough
- How to measure, stir, and bake

Materials List

- 1 cup peanut butter
- 1 cup light corn syrup
- 1¼ cups dry powdered milk
- 1½ cups sifted confectioners sugar
- A large bowl and a wooden spoon
- Paper plates and pencils

Directions

Help the children measure the peanut butter, corn syrup, dry powdered milk, and confectioners' sugar into the large bowl. They can take turns stirring with the wooden spoon until everything is mixed and a stiff dough forms.

Give everyone a paper plate and a pencil. Each child should write his or her name on the bottom of the plate. Make sure they hold their pencils correctly and use uppercase and lowercase letters.

Put a portion of dough on each plate. The children can shape it into bite-sized balls by pinching off pieces and rolling them between their hands.

Smaller children who cannot make balls can make snakes. Then they can cut the snakes into segments with a table knife to make bite-sized pieces.

Leave the Peanut Butter Balls on the children's plates and refrigerate them until firm, about 1 hour.

April

April is a time for making springtime projects of chicks, eggs, baskets—and, of course, bunnies! In this chapter there are four bunny projects, where children can create their own bunnies for Easter using such items as paper cups, newspapers, and blown-out eggs. As the children create with things found around the house and outside, they begin looking at common, everday items from a creative viewpoint. With the help of Craft-training, they begin to ask, "What can I turn *that* into?"

An added plus in spring is that children can go outdoors and find all sorts of natural objects, such as pinecones, to use in their crafts. Take the kids out on nature walks and encourage them to search out things to use creatively. Not only will they be learning to be innovative, the materials they find won't cost you a penny.

Of course, one *indoor* springtime activity that all kids love is making Easter eggs. Every year we dye tabletops, clothes, and half the kitchen while coloring a few dozen eggs. Then, on Easter morning, no one wants to eat the eggs whose whites look like large bruises. I make these eggs into egg salad, along with the ones that someone sat on because the Easter Bunny hid them under the couch cushions.

Craft-Training Skills to Learn

Use April crafts to teach the following skills:

- Learning the names of colors
- Learning the names of shapes
- How to cut, glue, paint, color, and tie a bow
- Understanding the meaning of *first*, *second*, *third*, etc.
- How to draw a face
- How to print his or her name
- Counting
- How to put things together
- How to follow directions
- Learning the meaning of *upside down*, *fold in half*, *insert*, *overlap*, *top of*, *middle*, and *between*
- How to work with dough

PLANTING SEEDS

The children can begin the spring season by planting seeds. One of the best to plant is the marigold. It sprouts easily, grows even if overwatered, and can be transplanted to the yard or a big flowerpot. It blooms all summer, and its seeds can be saved for next year.

Beans are good plants to grow, too. The children can plant the dried beans that are sold in the grocery store for cooking. Within two weeks they will sprout and grow leaves. Beans aren't likely to grow seed pods indoors, but the plants grow fast, they grow big, and children like them.

Skills to Teach

Teach children 2 years old and up:

- To count to 5
- How seeds change into plants
- That plants need water and sun to grow
- The three parts of a plant; the leaves, the roots, and the stem

Materials List

- A Styrofoam drinking cup for each child
- A plastic coffee can lid or shortening lid for each child
- Crayons or water-based markers
- Potting soil
- Marigold seeds or any dried beans

Directions

Give each child a Styrofoam drinking cup. They can decorate it with crayons or markers.

Poke a small hole in the bottom of the cups for drainage. Use the plastic lids as drip trays under the cups.

Fill the cups three-quarters full of potting soil. Give each child five seeds. Say to them, "Let's see how many seeds you have. Can you count them with me?" Count the seeds out loud with them, then ask, "How many seeds do you have? That's right. You have *five* seeds."

The children should plant the seeds in the cups, covering them lightly with 1/4 inch of soil. Help them water their seeds and place them in a sunny window. Talk with them about the fact that seeds need sun and water to grow.

Make sure that they water the seeds often enough to keep the soil moist. After about two weeks the seeds have sprouted enough to show plant growth.

Pull up one of the plants when it is a few inches tall. Wash the dirt off so your children can examine the *roots*, the *stem*, and the *leaves*. Explain that the plant's *roots* drink water from the dirt. The *leaves* make food for the plant when the sun shines on them. Without water, the plant would dry up. Without sun, the plant would not be able to make food.

Each week pull up another plant until only one strong plant remains growing in each cup.

PAPER CUP BUNNY

Any plain white paper cup will do for this craft. Generic cups make very good bunnies (FIG. 4-1).

Skills to Teach

Teach children 2 years old and up:

- The color *pink*
- How to draw a face
- The meaning of *upside down* and *fold in half*

Teach children 4 years old and up cutting skills.

Materials List

- A plain white paper cup for each bunny
- Permanent markers in two or three different colors
- Pink construction paper
- A white paper napkin for each bunny
- Cotton balls
- Scissors
- A small stapler (optional)

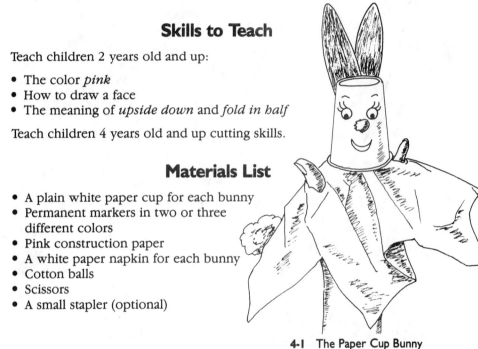

4-1 The Paper Cup Bunny

Directions

Give each child a cup and tell them to turn the cups *upside down*. Help each child draw eyes and a mouth on his or her cup, using permanent markers. Supervise closely since these markers don't wash off.

Trace and cut out two ears from pink paper for each bunny (FIG. 4-2). Children 4 years old and up can cut their own, but you should do the cutting for a younger child. Help them glue the *pink* ears to the back of the Bunny's head, or staple them on with the small stapler.

Use a sharp pencil to make a hole in each cup where the nose should be. Make the hole small, just big enough for the tip of the child's finger.

Use a white napkin for each dress. Show your children how to *fold* the napkin *in half*. Cut three small holes on the fold (FIG. 4-2).

Your children can glue a cotton ball to the back of the napkin dress for a bunny tail.

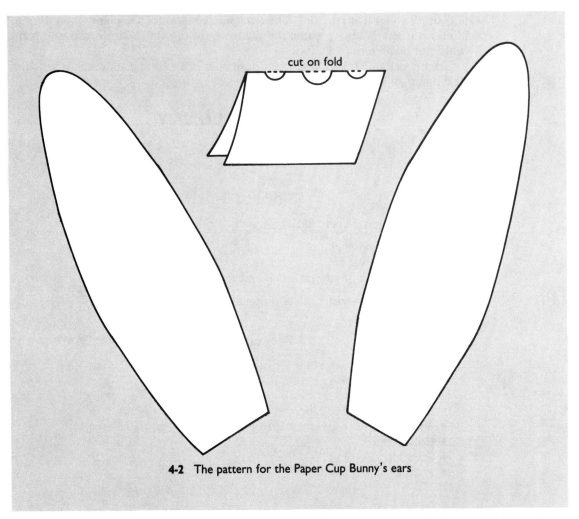

cut on fold

4-2 The pattern for the Paper Cup Bunny's ears

To make the Paper Cup Bunny work as a puppet, a child can stick his pointer finger through the middle hole in the napkin, then poke the finger through the hole in the cup to make the Bunny's nose. He can stick his thumb through one of the remaining napkin holes, and his pinkie finger through the other hole to make paws.

Children can make "designer dresses" for their puppets by decorating different napkins with water-based markers. (Be sure to put newspaper under their work.) They can even make a wedding veil by putting a napkin over the Bunny's ears.

BUNNY BAG

Girls fill their bags with everything from doll clothes to secret messages. Boys usually fill their bags with little cars (FIG. 4-3).

Skills to Teach

Teach children 2 years old and up:

- The color *yellow*
- The *rectangle* shape
- How to draw a face
- How to write his or her name

Teach children 4 years old and up:

- Cutting and gluing skills
- How to put something together (assembling skills)
- The meaning of *overlap*

Materials List

- Two sheets of yellow construction paper for each child
- A ruler and pencil
- Scissors
- Glue
- Transparent tape
- A paper punch
- Water-based markers or crayons
- Yarn 24 inches long or longer
- Cotton balls

4-3 A Bunny Bag

Directions

For each bag, use a pencil and ruler and draw a 6½-×-12-inch rectangle on yellow paper. See A in FIG. 4-4. Draw another rectangle 4 × 12 inches on yellow paper. (See B.) This second rectangle is the Bunny's head. To make his ears, draw a 5½-inch V shape in one end of rectangle (B), as shown in FIG. 4-4. Round off the tips of the ears.

Cut these shapes out for younger children; those 4 years old and up can cut their own.

Help the children position the head (B) halfway down rectangle (A), as shown in C in FIG. 4-4, and glue in place. Next they should *overlap* and glue the edges of (A), forming a cylinder with the head *inside* it. Press the bottom of the cylinder together and tape it securely to form a bag.

The children can draw rabbit faces on the Bunny Bags, as shown in FIG. 4-3.

Use the paper punch to make two holes in the back of each bag, near the top, one on each side of the Bunny's head.

Tie a yarn handle through the holes to make a shoulder bag. A 2- or 3-year-old needs a 24-inch long handle. Bigger children need bigger handles.

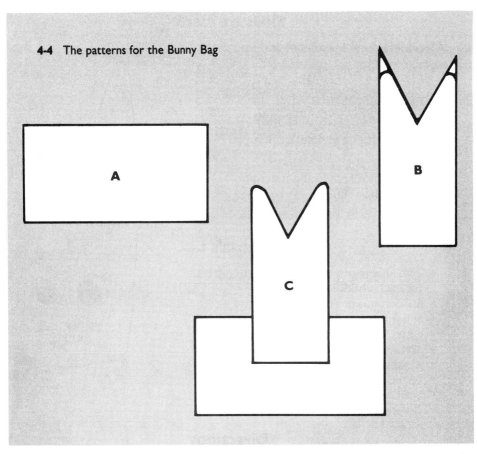

4-4 The patterns for the Bunny Bag

Tell the children to print their names on the front of the Bunny Bag. Help them do this neatly, making sure they hold the crayon or marker correctly. They should use uppercase and lowercase letters.

The bag can be left plain, or it can be decorated with crayons, markers, or cutout flowers.

The children can glue a cotton ball on the back for a tail.

woolie-pullie

It's very important to talk to your children while they are making crafts. Follow the conversation guidewords in italics if you wish. Be very precise in describing all craft items in terms of numbers, shapes, and color.

PINECONE FUNNY BUNNY

Many areas of the country have pine trees. If there are any near you, pick up the cones and dry them in a paper bag for a week. Then use them to make Pinecone Funny Bunnies (FIG. 4-5).

Skills to Teach

Teach children 2 years old and up:

- The colors *black*, *white*, and *pink*
- Gluing skills

Teach children 4 years old and up:

- Cutting skills
- How to put something together
- The meaning of *first* through *eighth*

Materials List

The first six items must be purchased in a craft or fabric store

- A 1¹/₂-inch white pom-pom for each child
- 3¹/₂-inch pink pom-pom for each child
- A ³/₈-inch black pom-pom for each child
- A 12-inch pipe cleaner for each child
- Movable paste-on eyes, size 10 mm, two for each child
- Pink felt
- Scissors
- Glue
- Cardboard
- A pinecone, 2 inches or taller for each child

4-5 The Pinecone Funny Bunny

Directions

Draw the Funny Bunny feet onto cardboard. Cut it out for younger children; encourage children 4 years old and up to cut their own. Draw two paws on the pink felt for each bunny and cut them out.

Give each child a pinecone, a foot, two paws, a white pom-pom, three pink pom-poms, a black pom-pom, a pipe cleaner, and two eyes. Then tell them the following:

"*First*, put the *white* pom-pom in the middle of the pipe cleaner."

"*Second*, cross the ends of the pipe cleaner over and twist the pipe cleaner tightly around the *white* pom-pom to hold it in place."

"*Third*, bend the ends of the pipe cleaner in half and twist them shut to form ears.

"*Fourth*, glue on the eyes, the *black* nose, and two *pink* pom-pom cheeks."

"*Fifth*, glue the head onto the top of the pinecone. If the pinecone is too pointed, break off the tip to make a place for gluing on the head.

"*Sixth*, glue the *pink* paws on the front of the pinecone."

"*Seventh*, glue the cardboard foot to the bottom of the pinecone so the Funny Bunny will stand up.

"*Eighth*, glue the last *pink* pom-pom to the back of the Pinecone Funny Bunny for a tail.''

Before using pinecones and seed pods for crafts, put them in a plastic bag and seal with a twist tie. Freeze them for three days to kill bugs that might be hiding in them.

PINECONE OWL

The youngest child can turn a pinecone into an owl by adding circles and triangles (FIG. 4-6).

Skills to Teach

Teach children 2 years old and up:

- The colors *green* and *yellow*
- The letter *O*
- The *circle* and *triangle* shapes
- The meaning of *large*, *small*, *top*, *center*, *inside*, and *below*

Materials List

- A pinecone. (I used a 5-inch pinecone.)
- Green and yellow construction paper
- Two notebook reinforcers
- A narrow black marker
- Scissors
- Glue

Directions

4-6 The Pinecone Owl

Use in the patterns in FIG. 4-7 to trace two green circles and two yellow triangles, plus yellow feet. Cut out the pieces. Give them to the child, along with a pinecone and glue.

Also give her two notebook reinforcers. Then tell her the following:

"Stick the letter *O* (a notebook reinforcer) in the *center* of each *green circle* eye. Use the marker to draw lines and an eyeball on each eye. Draw the eyeball *inside* the letter *O*.

"Glue the *green circle* eyes close together near the *top* of the pinecone.

"The *small yellow triangle* is the owl's beak. Draw two dots on the *triangle* for nose holes so the owl can breathe. Glue the beak *below* the *circle* eyes.

"The *large yellow triangle* is the owl's tail. Draw some lines on it. Glue the tail on the back of the owl with the wide end of the *triangle* hanging down.

"Put glue on the *yellow* feet. Set the owl on the feet and let him stay there until the glue dries."

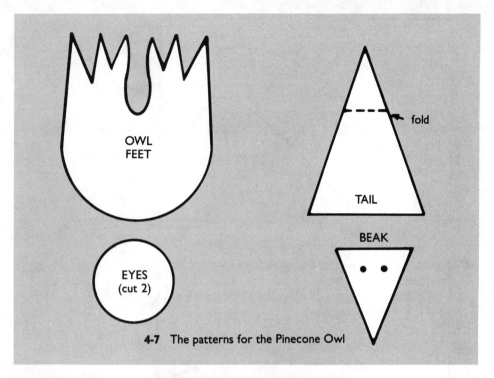

4-7 The patterns for the Pinecone Owl

NEWSPAPER BUNNIES

Decorate a string of dancing bunnies for a springtime door or window (FIG. 4-8).

Skills to Teach

Teach children 2 years old and up:

- How to draw faces and coloring skills
- To count to *8*

Teach children 4 years old and up cutting skills.

4-8 Newspaper Bunnies

place on fold

4-9 The pattern for Newspaper Bunnies

Materials List

- A large sheet of newspaper for every two bunnies
- Water-based markers and crayons
- Scissors
- Transparent tape

Directions

Fold each sheet of newspaper into one-quarter its original size. Now fold it into 3¹/₄-inch-wide pleats.

For each child, trace a Bunny pattern in FIG. 4-9 on the folded paper so that the middle of the rabbit, as well as its ear, paw, and foot are laying against the folds. Do not cut these folds.

Cut out the Bunny through all layers of newspaper. Children 4-years-old and up can try cutting their own, but will need help. Unfold. You have made eight Bunnies, enough for two children.

Say to the children, "Look how many bunnies we have! Let's count them to see how many there are." Count the Bunnies out loud with the children. Then ask, "How many bunnies are there? *Eight!* There are *eight* Newspaper Bunnies."

The children should decorate their Bunnies with crayons or markers, trying to make each one different from the next, and drawing a face on each. When they are finished, you can tape the Bunnies together into a long line before hanging them up for display.

PAPER-STRIP NOSEGAY

These paper flowers (FIG. 4-10) in a bright display will delight any child. And, they are easy to make.

Skills to Teach

Teach children 3 years old and up:

- How to cut on a line
- How to glue

Teach children 4 years old and up:

- How to fold paper and doilies *in half*
- To follow directions
- Counting to *18*

Materials List

- Two sheets of 9-×-12-inch green construction paper
- Construction paper in assorted colors for flowers
- Ruler
- Pencil

- Scissors
- Glue
- Cellophane tape
- 12-inch paper doily with a solid center
- Ribbon

Directions

Instruct the children as follows:

"Fold each sheet of green paper *in half* crosswise. Use a pencil and ruler to draw 1-inch cutting lines 4 inches long on the folded edge. Cut on these lines."

You must do the drawing and cutting for very young children, but encourage children 3 years old and older to at least try cutting on the lines.

Then continue by saying, "The cuts make nine flower stems on each paper. Leave the papers folded in half. Lay one paper on top of the other. Roll them up into a cylinder. Tape the bottom so it can't unroll.

"Separate the stems by gently bending them outward, one at a time.

"Use the pattern in FIG. 4-11 to trace and draw eighteen flowers from paper of several colors. Cut them out. Use a paper punch to make dozens of tiny circles from paper scraps. Glue several of these circles in the center of each flower. Glue one flower on the end of each stem.

"Draw a two-inch *X* in the center of the doily. Cut the *X*. Stick the bottom of the nosegay through this opening. Tape the doily in place. Squeeze the doily gently up around the flowers. Add a strip of tape around the bottom of the doily to hold it up in this position.

"Tie a ribbon around the bottom of the nosegay. Stick a piece of tape on the ribbon to keep it from slipping off the bottom."

4-10 The Paper-Strip Nosegay

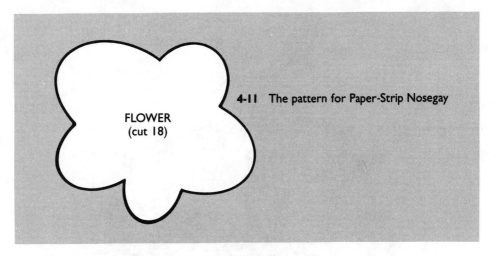

FLOWER
(cut 18)

4-11   The pattern for Paper-Strip Nosegay

___woolie-pullie___

To cut a pattern for many children at the same time, staple the layers of construction paper together. When you cut, the layers won't slide apart.

EGG CARTON BASKET

Another way to prepare your children for Easter by helping them make Egg Carton Baskets. You can make three baskets from each egg carton if you cut carefully (FIG. 4-12).

Skills to Teach

Teach children 2 years old and up:

- Drawing skills
- The letter *U*

Teach children 4 years old and up:

- The meaning of *first* through *sixth*
- How to tie a bow

Materials List

- Styrofoam egg cartons
- Pipe cleaners
- Narrow ribbon
- Easter grass
- Jelly beans
- Scissors
- Water-based markers and a ballpoint pen

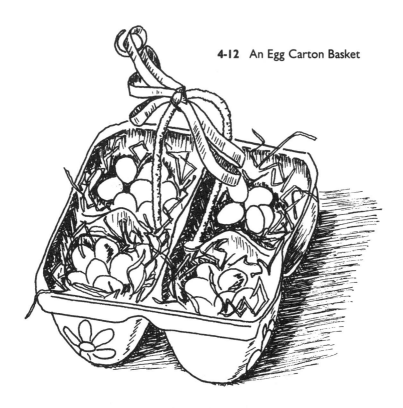

Directions

Cut the lids off the egg cartons. Discard them or give them to the children to use as a sandbox toy. They also make nice boats for small dollies in the bathtub.

Cut the remaining part of the cartons into three baskets of four eggcups each. Trim with scissors to make them look neat. Give each child a basket, a pipe cleaner, and a 10-inch piece of narrow ribbon.

Help the children follow these directions:

"*First*, bend the pipe cleaner so that it looks like the letter *U*.

"*Second*, push the sharp ends of the pipe cleaner through the top of the Styrofoam egg basket, about one inch apart.

"*Third*, turn the basket over, and bend the two ends of the pipe cleaner to make a tiny foot on each one.

"*Fourth*, turn the basket back over. Pull the handle up gently until the feet catch and hold.

"*Fifth*, decorate the basket." Give them water-based markers and a ballpoint pen.

"*Sixth*, tie the ribbon into a bow on the handle."

Fill the eggcups with a little bit of Easter grass and lots of jelly beans. If you snip the grass into short bits with scissors, it stays in the basket better and is easier to vacuum off the floor.

TWELVE BLOWN-OUT EGGS

Start saving those eggshells by leaving them whole! Follow these directions to blow raw eggs into a bowl whenever you are cooking with eggs. Run water into the empty shells and let them drain. Then store them in an egg carton. If your family likes scrambled eggs or french toast, or if you do a lot of baking, it won't take long to collect several dozen empty shells (FIG. 4-13).

Skills to Teach

Teach children 2 years old and up:

- To count to *4*
- To count to *12*
- How to draw a face
- How to paint
- Gluing skills

Teach children 4 years old and up:

- How many make a dozen
- How to cut, glue, and create

Materials List

- Old newspapers to cover your kitchen table
- 12 large raw eggs in an egg carton for each child
- Water colors and brushes
- Cups or bowls for rinse water.
  (Use ones that do not tip easily.)
- Two cardboard toilet-paper rolls for each child
- Cotton balls
- Narrow-tipped water-based markers
- Scissors
- Glue
- Yellow yarn
- Ballpoint pen
- White paper

Directions

Using a corsage pin or some other sharp instrument, poke a hole in one end of a raw egg. Carefully take away bits of shell to widen the hole to about 1/8 inch.

Stick a pin or a toothpick into the opening and stir the raw egg inside the shell to break the yolk so it can be blown through the hole.

Now make a tiny hole in the other end of the egg. Put this end tightly against your mouth and blow into the egg, forcing the insides to come out. Hold the egg over a bowl to keep scrambled egg off your kitchen counter.

When the shell is empty, run a stream of water into the egg and shake it dry. Continue with all 12 eggs. Store them in an egg carton until you are ready to work with the children.

4-13 Blown-Out Eggs

Spread newspapers on the table and put a painting coat on each child. Give each child four of the eggs.

Say to them, "Here are some eggs for you to paint. How many do you have? Let's count them." Count the eggs out loud with them. Then ask, "How many eggs do you have? *Four*! You have *four* eggs to paint."

Give them the watercolors, a brush, and a shallow cup of water. Show them how to rub the wet brush on the paint and transfer the color to the egg. Show them how to rinse their brushes so that the colors do not mix together.

They can paint the eggs in any combination of varied hues that suits their fancy. When they are finished with each one, set it in the egg carton to dry.

Put away the paints and rinse water. Give each child four more eggs and a set of water-based markers. Again help them count the eggs out loud. Then they can color the eggs all over with the markers. Stripes, dots, swirls, and other designs are easy to add with markers since the colors don't run together. Put them in the egg carton to dry, also.

Give them the last four eggs, two toilet-paper rolls, scissors, glue, yellow yarn, a ballpoint pen, and white paper. Help them count the *four* eggs out loud.

Cut the toilet-paper rolls into four cylinders 1½ inches high. Your children should set the eggs in these.

To make a girl, cut the yarn into 16 strands 2½ inches long. The children can spread glue on the top of one egg and down the sides a bit. Then they can lay eight pieces of yarn on each side of the doll's head, adding more glue if necessary to make it stick. Help them tie this yarn hair loosely together at the bottom with more yarn to make ponytails.

They can draw a face on the egg, using narrow-tipped markers. They can draw arms on the cardboard roll with the ballpoint pen, and can decorate the roll to look like a dress.

To make a rabbit, trace the ears onto white paper (FIG. 4-14). Cut them out for younger children. Encourage those 4 years old and up to cut their own.

Your children can draw a face on an egg with a narrow-tipped marker. To make it look like a rabbit, they can add a triangle nose and whiskers. They should color the ears *pink*, and then glue them on the back of the rabbit's head.

They can draw paws and feet on the cardboard roll with the ballpoint pen. Then they can color the roll pink with a marker. A cotton ball can be glued on for a tail.

Repeat with the last two eggs to make another person and another rabbit, or let them make their own creations.

When all 12 eggs are decorated, admire them with your children and count them out loud together. Then ask, "How many eggs did you decorate? *12*! You decorated a *dozen* eggs."

woolie-pullie

Children enjoy playing with blown-out eggs, pretending they have real eggs to "cook" with. When the shells break, the pieces sweep up easily.

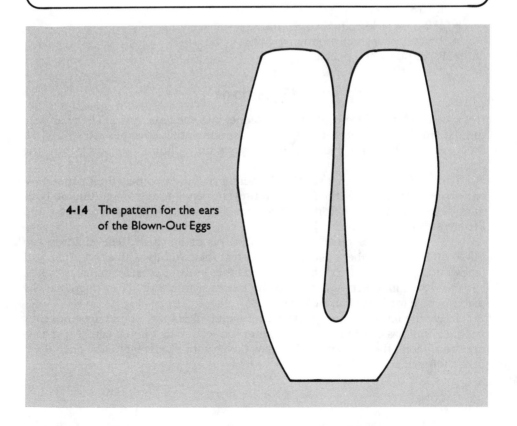

4-14 The pattern for the ears of the Blown-Out Eggs

EASTER MINTS

This is a no-cook recipe the children can mix with their hands. Flavor it with any of the liquid flavorings in the supermarket, such as strawberry or lemon.

If you want, you can divide the mixture into three portions and add a few drops of food coloring to tint it yellow, red, and green. Then knead a small amount of a different flavoring into each one. This recipe makes about $1^1/_2$ pounds of candy.

Skills to Teach

Teach children 2 years old and up:

- To sit still, listen, and follow directions
- How to shape the dough
- How to print his or her name

Materials List

- $1/_3$ cup soft butter
- $1/_3$ cup light corn syrup
- $1/_2$ teaspoon salt
- 1 teaspoon flavoring
- $3^1/_2$ cups (1 lb.) sifted confectioner's sugar
- A large bowl and a wooden spoon
- Paper plates and pencils

Directions

Help the children measure all the ingredients into the large bowl. They can take turns stirring the mixture with the wooden spoon until it becomes too stiff. Then they can knead it with their hands. They should continue kneading until the dough is smooth.

Give each child a paper plate and a pencil. Tell them to turn their plates *over* and write their names on the *bottom* to prevent pencil lead from getting on their mints. Help them hold their pencils correctly. Make sure they use uppercase and lowercase letters.

Give each child a portion of dough on his or her plate. The children can pinch off pieces, roll them into balls, and press them *lightly* with a fork to make a fancy butter mint. Children who cannot roll the candy into balls can make snakes, cut the snakes into pieces, and press the pieces with a fork. They might eat the pieces with a fork, but that's okay too.

Leave the mints on the plates and refrigerate them for 30 minutes until they become firm. Easter Mints taste even better the second day, if you can keep everyone from eating them all on the first day. Cover with plastic wrap and keep them in the refrigerator.

May

Children can usually work outside during May, so painting crafts that teach color, method, and creativity are assembled in one chapter. Three puppet crafts teach everyone to follow directions while learning some very specific terms such as *above*, *larger*, *smaller*, and *first*, *second*, *third*, and so on.

May Clay Play

Modeling clay is like bubble gum. It's a wonderful thing for children to have, but it ruins the rug and the furniture, sticks to your shoes, and ends up stamped into the linoleum or stuck to the wallpaper.

By all means don't let this problem keep you from buying clay for your children. As with other crafts, you must first set rules and limits. Cut up an old plastic tablecloth into mats and give one to each child; discarded plastic place mats work fine, too. Seat the children at a table in the backyard. Show them how to roll, squeeze, and pinch the clay into shapes, but don't let them throw it at each other.

When they tire of the clay, save their creative pieces on a paper plate for a few days to admire them. Store the clay in a clean coffee can with a lid on it and save the mats.

Craft-Training Skills to Learn

Craft-training skills to practice in May repeat the same skills of past months. Children need to repeat to learn. May projects teach them the same things, but in a fresh way with each different craft.

May Craft-training skills include:

- Learning the names of colors
- Gluing, coloring, cutting, and lacing skills, which emphasize eye-hand coordination and small motor skills
- How to read and write his or her name
- Learning the basic geometric shapes
- Learning the meaning of *above*, *on top of*, *larger*, *smaller*
- Learning the meaning of *first* through *ninth*

MOTHER'S DAY PLATE OF PROMISES

Ever since Anna Jarvis of West Virginia originated Mother's Day on May 10, 1908, we have tried to make this day special for mothers. Stores are loaded with Mother's Day cards and presents, but nothing is quite as special as a gift made by a child who obviously adores you (FIG. 5-1).

Skills to Teach

Teach children 2 years old and up:

- Gluing skills
- Coloring skills
- Lacing
- How to write "MOM"

Teach children 4 years old and up:

- Cutting skills
- To think of nice things to do for another person

Materials List

- Paper plates (Generic plates work very nicely)
- Water-based markers or crayons
- A hole puncher
- A colorful magazine
- Scissors
- Glue
- Narrow crimped paper ribbon
- A sheet of white paper and a pen

Directions

Fold a paper plate in half. Cut it on the fold. Give each child one and one-half plates.

Turn the half plate upside down, so children can decorate them using water-based markers or crayons. Flower shapes can be cut from construction paper or from brightly colored magazine pages. They can glue these shapes on the plates and draw stems and leaves with a green marker.

Lay the half plate upside down on the whole plate, lining up the edges. Punch two holes through both plates with the hole puncher, making one hole on each side of the half plate, near the top. Tie ribbons through the two holes to anchor the half plate in position.

Now use the hole puncher to make holes 1 inch apart all the way around the plate, punching through both plates when necessary.

Starting at the top of the plate, the children can thread ribbon in and out of the holes all the way around. Tie the ribbon into a loop at the top so the plate can be hung.

5-1 The Mother's Day Plate of Promises

Help each child think of ways in which he or she can help Mommy. Some of those ways might be: "dust the living room," "make my bed," "feed the dog," "dry the dishes," "clean my room," "sweep the porch," or anything else the child can actually do.

As the child tells you his own promises, print each one on a separate strip of paper. Let the child put his promises inside his plate. Make sure he understands that his mother can give him a strip whenever she chooses, and he must do the task that is written on it.

Help the children write "MOM" on the front of their plates with a pen or marker. Make sure they hold the pen the right way when writing.

CRAYON BATIK

For this craft, the children draw a design with crayon, and then wad it into a ball. They are always pleased and surprised at the final result (FIG. 5-2).

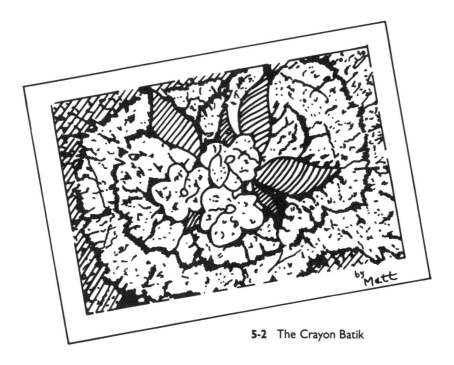

5-2 The Crayon Batik

Skills to Teach

Teach children 8 and up:

- The meaning of *batik* (buh ték)
- The importance of following directions
- A different and interesting art technique

Materials List

- Newspaper to spread on the work area
- White construction paper
- Crayons
- A dishpan or bucket for water
- Paper towels
- Black tempera paint thinned with water
- A Styrofoam meat tray
- A household sponge cut into 1-inch squares
- Larger sheets of colored construction paper for mounting
- Glue

Directions

Tell the children that the *batik* method comes from Indonesia. Usually it's used to print a design on cloth by coating the parts not to be dyed with wax. The children will coat their paper with wax (a crayon drawing) and then create cracks and crevices for the dye (tempera paint).

First, they should cover their work area with newspapers. Tell them to use crayons only, no pencils, to draw a picture of anything they wish. The batik will turn out best if the picture is large without a lot of detail. They should color every bit of the paper (one side only) with thick, heavy crayon.

Now, they must wad their picture into a ball. This instruction always surprises the children, who have always been told not to wrinkle their beautiful drawings! Tell them not to roll, fold, or tear it; just wad it up like a softball.

Tell them to dip the wadded picture into a pan of water, give it one more squeeze, and carefully spread it out on paper towels. They should pat it with more towels to remove excess water.

Pour a little thinned black tempera paint into a Styrofoam tray. Give each child a 1-inch piece of sponge. They should dip the sponge in the paint and smooth it over their entire picture.

The black paint will be absorbed only by the wrinkles in the paper; the wax crayon will resist the paint.

Lay the paintings flat overnight to dry. Use glue to mount each one on a larger sheet of colored paper.

PAPIER-MÂCHÉ PIÑATA

This will be a very nonmessy project if you give each child her own small bowl of paste and her own balloon (FIG. 5-3).

Skills to Teach

Teach children 5 years old and up:

- How to create with papier-mâché

Materials List

- Newspaper to cover worksurface
- Newspaper cut or torn into 1-inch strips
- 9-inch balloon for each child
- Large bowl
- Wire whisk
- A small bowl for each child's paste
- Flour
- Water
- Four 10-inch pieces of ribbon or string for each child
- A roll of strapping tape (Found in the stationery section of grocery and drug stores.)
- Tissue wrapping paper in two different colors
- Ruler
- Scissors
- Glue in a small squeeze bottle

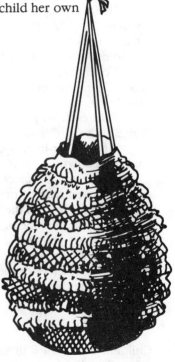

5-3 The Papier-Mâché Piñata

Directions

Cover each tabletop with layers of newspaper. Each child should wear something to cover up his clothes. You should, too!

Blow up the balloon and knot it shut. Make paste by mixing 1½ cups flour and 1 cup water with the wire whisk in a large bowl. Make more as it is needed. A 5-pound bag of flour makes enough paste for about 25 piñatas. Give each child a bowl of paste and a balloon, plus a supply of newspaper strips. Then tell them the following:

"Tear your newspaper strips into three-inch pieces. Dip a strip into the paste. Gently pull the strip between your fingers to remove the extra paste."

"Smooth the strip onto the balloon. Repeat this step until the entire balloon is covered, except for the end where it is knotted. Leave a small opening at that end."

"Cover your balloon with a second layer of paste strips. Make sure they are smooth."

"Now add a top layer of *dry* newspaper strips. Make sure the surface is smooth. Put your piñata aside to dry for several days."

When the piñatas have *completely* dried, you may continue:

"Pop the balloon inside your piñata by cutting the tied end with scissors. Pull out the balloon and throw it away."

"Trim the opening with scissors until it is about two inches wide."

"Use strapping tape to fasten one end of a ribbon on the outside of the piñata opening. Tape the other ribbons evenly around the opening in the same way. Pull the four ribbons up above the piñata and tie them together to make a handle."

To decorate the piñatas, tell the children the following:

"Cover your work area with newspapers. Choose two colors of wrapping paper. Cut the paper into strips three inches wide. Use the ruler to help with this step."

"Fold each strip in half lengthwise so it is one and one-half inches wide. Fringe each strip by snipping it with scissors *on the folded edge*."

"Glue a four-inch square of tissue on the bottom of the piñata to cover it. Smooth it down."

"Just above this piece of tissue, spread a thin line of glue around the piñata. Glue a fringed strip of one color tissue all the way around the piñata, with the fringe hanging toward the bottom."

"Spread a thin line of glue above the top of this fringe. Now add a fringe of a different color, gluing it all the way around the piñata."

The children should continue alternating tissue strips of two colors until the piñata is completely decorated. Let the glue dry overnight. The piñatas may be filled with candy, or they may be used as a trinket basket in a child's room.

STRAW PAINTING

Children can create a unique design with just some paint, paper, and a drinking straw. They'll blow through the straw and chase the paint all over the paper to create a picture that is different each time (FIG. 5-4).

5-4 Straw Painting

Skills to Teach

Teach children 2 years old and up:

- The names of colors
- How to write his or her name

Teach children 4 years old and up how to create a different effect with paint.

Materials List

- Newspapers to cover the table
- Painting coats
- Drawing or typing paper
- Pencils
- Drinking straws
- Thinned tempera paint. (Add water to thin it.)
- A teaspoon

Directions

Cover the table with newspapers. Roll up your children's sleeves and put a painting coat on them.

Give each child paper, a pencil, and a drinking straw and ask them to write their names on the paper. Make sure they use uppercase and lowercase letters, and that they hold their pencils correctly.

Pour a small amount of thinned paint into a teaspoon. Then pour the teaspoonful on a child's paper. As you give each child the paint, tell them its color. "Barbara, this is *purple* paint. What color is it? That's right: it's *purple*."

Tell her to aim the straw at the *purple* paint and blow hard. She can chase the little rivulets of paint all over the paper by blowing through the straw.

Next pour a different color in the teaspoon and put this on each child's paper. Tell the child the color. "Now let's add *yellow*. What color is this? That's right; it's *yellow*. The child can blow the yellow paint around on the paper in the same way.

Add more colors if you wish, telling the children the name of the color each time.

CLYDE THE CAT

Paper bags make great puppets and the children will enjoy turning them into a variety of creatures, such as Clyde the Cat (FIG. 5-5).

5-5 Clyde the Cat and Charlie Chicken

Skills to Teach

Teach children 2 years old and up:

- The colors *black*, *white*, *red*, *green*, *yellow*, and *pink*
- The *circle* and *triangle* shapes
- Gluing skills
- The meaning of *on top of*, *above*, *insert*, *larger*, and *smaller*

Teach children 4 years old and up:

- Cutting skills
- To follow directions
- The meaning of *first* through *seventh*

Materials List

- Two brown paper lunch bags for each puppet
- Black, red, green, yellow, and white construction paper
- A pink marker or crayon
- A black marker or pen
- Scissors
- Glue

Directions

For each puppet, use FIG. 5-6 to trace the following pieces on the construction paper: two white eyes, two green eyeballs, a red mouth, a black nose, and two yellow paws. Trace two ears and a tail on the second lunch bag. Cut all these pieces out for younger children. Encourage children 4 years old and up to cut their own.

Give each child a paper lunch bag and a set of Clyde the Cat pieces. Then tell them the following:

"*First*, glue the *white circle* eyes on the bottom of the closed bag.

"*Second*, glue the *green* eyeballs *on top of* the *white circles*.

"*Third*, glue the two *triangles* on Clyde's head for ears. Use the *pink* marker or crayon to color the ears *pink*.

"*Fourth*, *insert* the *red* mouth as far as it will go under the paper bag flap. Glue it in place.

"*Fifth*, glue the *black* nose between Clyde's eyes and one-quarter inch from the edge of the flap. With a *black* marker or pen, draw eyelashes above Clyde's eyes. Draw a straight line one-quarter inch long from the bottom of the nose to the edge of the flap. Cut a few skinny whiskers from *black* paper and glue them on both sides of the nose." You will need to help them with the measurements.

"*Sixth*, glue the two *yellow* paws on the front of Clyde, near the bottom.

"*Seventh*, glue Clyde's tail on his back. Make it stick out by folding down a one-quarter-inch flap on the end and putting glue on that flap only."

The children can make the puppet work by inserting their hand in the bag and bending their fingers so they fit into the flap. They can move their fingers up and down to make Clyde talk.

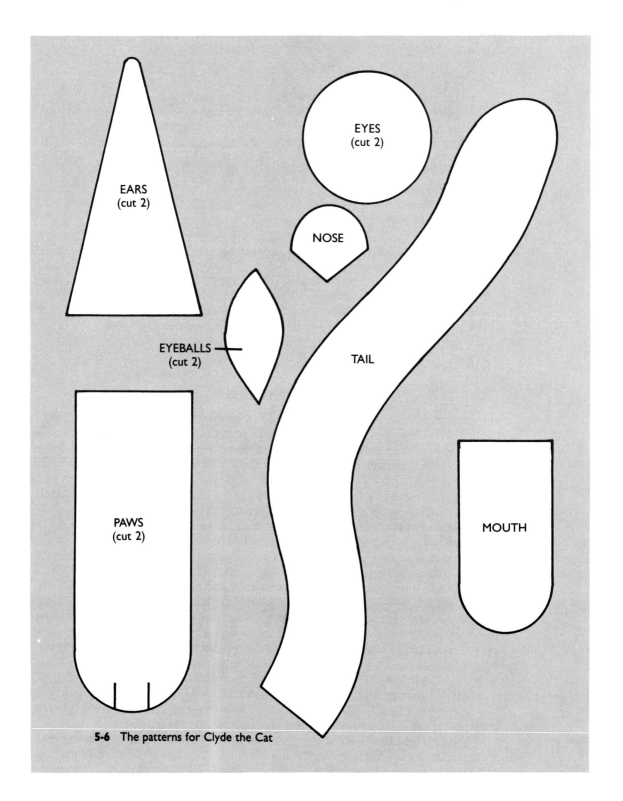

5-6 The patterns for Clyde the Cat

CHARLIE CHICKEN

Another puppet the children will enjoy making is Charlie Chicken (FIG. 5-6).

Skills to Teach

Teach children 2 years old and up:

- The colors *black*, *red*, *yellow*, and *white*
- The *triangle* and *circle* shapes
- The meaning of *on top of*, *above*, *insert*, *larger*, and *smaller*
- Gluing skills

Teach children 4 years old and up:

- Cutting skills
- To follow directions
- The meaning of *first* through *ninth*

Materials List

- Two brown paper lunch bags for each puppet
- Black, red, yellow, and white construction paper
- Scissors
- Glue

Directions

For each puppet, use FIG. 5-7 to trace the following pieces on the construction paper: two black eyeballs, two white eyes, a red comb and red tongue, a yellow top beak and bottom beak, and two yellow feet. Trace the tail and two wings on the second paper bag. Cut all these pieces out for younger children. Encourage children 4 years old and up to cut their own.

Give each child a paper lunch bag and a set of Charlie Chicken pieces. Then tell them the following:

"*First*, glue the *white circle* eyes on the bottom of the closed bag.

"*Second*, glue the *black circle* eyeballs *on top of* the *white circles*.

"*Third*, glue the *red* comb *above* Charlie Chicken's eyes.

"*Fourth*, *insert* the *larger yellow triangle* as far as it will go under the paper bag flap. Glue it in place.

"*Fifth*, *insert* the *red triangle* under the flap as far as it will go. Glue it *on top of* the *yellow triangle* to make a tongue.

"*Sixth*, glue the *smaller yellow triangle on top of* the paper bag flap. Make sure it is even with the *larger yellow triangle*, forming a beak. Draw two dots for nose holes.

"*Seventh*, glue the two *yellow* feet on the front of Charlie, near the bottom.

"*Eighth*, glue two wings on the front of Charlie, *above* his feet. Let them stick out so he can fly.

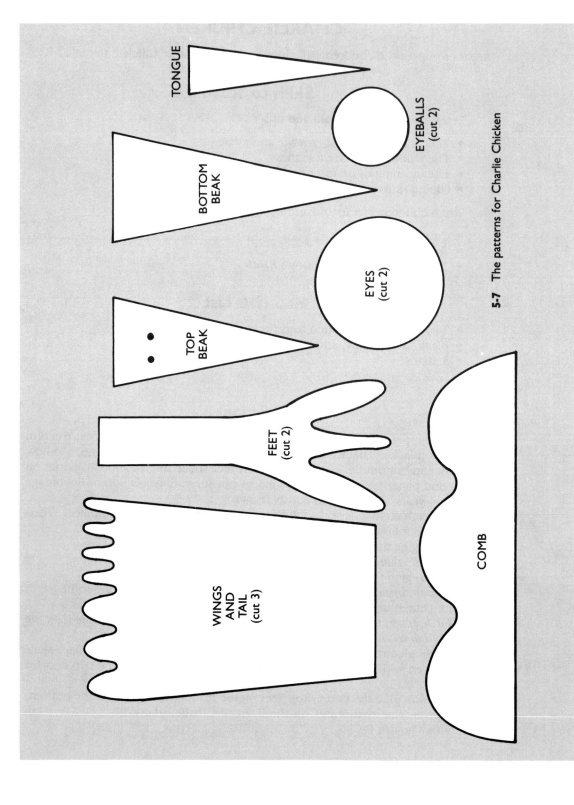

TONGUE

BOTTOM BEAK

EYEBALLS (cut 2)

EYES (cut 2)

TOP BEAK

FEET (cut 2)

WINGS AND TAIL (cut 3)

COMB

5-7 The patterns for Charlie Chicken

"*Ninth*, glue Charlie's tail on his back. Make it stick out by folding down a one-quarter-inch flap on the end and putting glue on that only." You will need to help with the measurements.

The children can make the puppet work by inserting their hand in the bag and bending their fingers so they fit into the flap. They can move their fingers up and down to make Charlie talk.

FINGER MOUSE

Another type of puppet children love is a finger puppet. Finger Mouse, shown in FIG. 5-8, will be sure to delight your children. One glove will make five mice.

Skills to Teach

Teach children 2 years old and up:

- Gluing skills
- Creative play with puppets

Teach children 4 years old and up cutting skills.

Materials List

- Two tiny movable paste-on eyes for each puppet. (They come in packs of 32 at craft stores.)
- A ladies dress glove
- Scissors that can cut cloth
- Lightweight yarn or string
- A black permanent marker
- A pink water-base marker or crayon
- Red felt
- Glue

Directions

Cut a 2-inch-long finger off the glove as shown in FIG. 5-8, also cutting a 2¹/4-inch-long tail down the back of the glove.

Put a Finger Mouse on each child's finger. Help them glue on two eyes.

They can use a black permanent marker to make a nose. Help them glue on a tiny piece of red felt for a tongue.

Help the children cut the yarn into ¹/2-inch pieces. They should glue two pieces on each side of the nose for whiskers.

Cut two ¹/2-inch rounded ears from the glove for each child. Hold them down tightly on a tabletop so the children can color one side of them with a pink marker or crayon. Help them glue them on the mouse's head just above its eyes. Press them with your finger so they stick up a little.

Slide the mouse off the children's fingers. Let them dry completely before the children play with them.

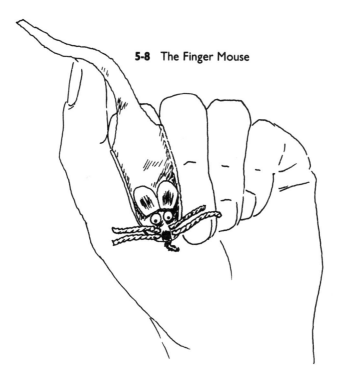

5-8 The Finger Mouse

PET PEBBLES

Children love to collect rocks and pebbles; so take them to a place where they can find a pebble to keep for a pet (FIG. 5-9). Parks and parking lots are good places to look.

Skills to Teach

Teach children 2 years old and up:

- The meaning of *small*
- Gluing skills
- To follow directions

Materials List

- A small, smooth pebble (about 1½ inch wide) for each child
- Two movable paste-on eyes for each child, size ⅜ inch
  (Buy them in a craft store.)
- Glue
- A small box and a piece of cotton ball for each child (optional)

5-9 Pet Pebbles

Directions

Each child should select a *small* smooth rock to take home. First, they must give their pet pebble a bath in the sink with soap and water. Dry it thoroughly with a paper towel or napkin.

Next, they must glue two eyes on their pebble so it can see.

If they have a small box, such as the kind jewelry comes in, they can use it for their pet's bed. Glue a wisp of cotton in the bottom of the box. Lay the pet pebble on it.

CORNFLAKE BALLS

This snack is a real treat for children. They can eat it warm or cold.

Skills to Teach

Teach children 2 years old and up:

- To sit still, listen, and follow directions
- How to read his or her name
- How to stir and measure

Materials List

- 1 cup peanut butter
- 1/2 cup honey
- 3 1/2 cups cornflakes
- A large bowl and a wooden spoon
- Paper plates and a marker
- Sesame seeds or wheat germ or finely ground nuts

Directions

Help the children measure the peanut butter and honey into a small pot. Stir constantly over medium heat until blended. Remove from heat.

Microwave Directions: The children can measure the peanut butter and honey into a large microwave bowl. Microwave on high for 1 minute. Remove from oven. Let the children stir until smooth.

Help the children measure and add 3½ cups of cornflakes. They can take turns stirring the mixture with a spoon.

If everyone is hungry and can't wait, give them a paper plate and a spoon and let them eat while it's warm.

To shape into balls, chill the dough for 30 minutes in the refrigerator. While the dough is chilling, play the Read-Your-Name Game (See ''November'' crafts.)

After the dough is stiff, put a portion on each child's plate. They can pinch off small pieces, roll them into balls, and then roll the balls in sesame seeds, wheat germ, or finely ground nuts.

Store these snacks in the refrigerator on the children's plates.

June

This chapter begins with a terrific Father's Day craft that is very hard to find in other craft books. It takes a week to complete, but fathers are worth it, so start early. Several old-fashioned crafts that children have learned from and enjoyed for generations are also among this month's crafts. Clothespin Dolls, Making Paste for Cut-and-Paste Pages, and Stocking Kitty have been around since grandmother's day, at least, and Making Butter has been around since cows were discovered.

Paste Is a Sticky Word

While teaching first grade, I met a young lady named Glenda who had a passion for paste—she liked to eat it. We used school-issue paste that was thick, slimy, white, and had a minty smell. Glenda would take giant fistfuls and hide it in her desk to nibble when I wasn't looking. At least homemade paste will not be harmful to anyone's health if you happen to have a paste-nibbler in your family.

Learning to paste isn't easy for very young children since they must spread the paste on the back of the picture. They often begin by spreading paste on the front of the picture, turning the picture over to stick it to their paper, and then wondering where their picture went.

Craft-Training Skills to Learn

For the first time in this book, the children are asked to print their last name as well as their first. They are introduced to *reading* the names of the five shapes, and to reading and spelling an important word to them: "DAD." Many of the crafts stress the importance of cooperating and taking turns, which they must do in school later.

Craft-training skills to practice in June include:

- How to paste
- Cutting, drawing, and lacing skills
- How to spread with a knife, another eye-hand coordination skill
- Learning the names of colors
- Learning the meaning of *divide*, *in half*, *larger* and *largest*, and *smaller* and *smallest*
- Counting
- Following directions
- Shaping dough
- Measuring
- How butter and peanut butter are made
- Creative play with clothespin dolls and egg carton caterpillars
- How to tie and braid (older children)

DAD GIFT FOR FATHER'S DAY

Start this craft (FIG. 6-1) about a week before Father's Day so that everything has time to dry. Sawdust makes a big mess in the kitchen, so plan on working in the garage or outside.

Skills to Teach

Teach children 2 years old and up:

- The colors *brown* and *blue*
- How many make *3*
- How to shape dough to form letters
- The letters *A* and *D*

Teach children 4 years old and up:

- The meaning of *divide*
- How to spell *DAD*

Materials List

Buy the first five items in a hardware store.

- A 1-×-4-×-6-inch piece of wood for each child
- Fine-grained sandpaper
- Wood stain, any color
- Clear shellac
- A 2-inch-wide paintbrush for each child
- An old piece of cloth for each child
- Flour-Salt Dough. (See "March Crafts.")
- Blue food coloring
- Contact cement (glue)

Directions

Give your children the wood and a piece of sandpaper. Show them how to rub the wood until it's smooth.

Spread newspapers on the work area. Put a painting coat on your children. Pour about a tablespoon of wood stain on an old piece of cloth. Give one to each child and let them rub the wood until it is colored *brown* all over.

Make Flour-Salt Dough and add a few drops of blue food coloring. Let the children knead the color into the dough. To teach the name of the color, ask them, "What color is the dough?" If they do not know, tell them. "It's *blue*." Then ask again, "What color is it? That's right. It's *blue*."

Give each child 1½ cups of blue dough. Tell them to *divide* it into three equal pieces. Ask your younger child how many pieces he has. If he does not know, count the pieces out loud with him. Then ask again, "How many pieces of dough do you have? Yes, you have *three* pieces."

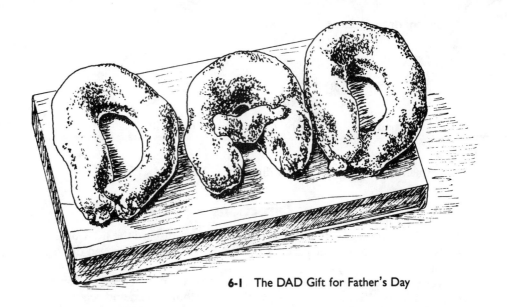

6-1 The DAD Gift for Father's Day

This step can be done at the kitchen table. Give each child a little flour to spread on the table in front of them. Help them roll the dough into three snakes, then curl and bend the snakes to form the letters *DAD*. Talk about the names of the letters and what they spell.

Arrange the letters on a cookie sheet covered with aluminum foil. Bake at 225°F until they are hard and dry, but not browned. You may want to leave them in a turned-off oven overnight to help them dry.

Help your children glue the baked letters onto the piece of wood, spelling *DAD*.

Go to the garage once more with old newspapers and painting coats. Give them a 2-inch brush and let them shellac the entire DAD Sign. Let them dry before giving them to Dad.

EGG CARTON CATERPILLAR

A fun craft to make is this Egg Carton Caterpillar (FIG. 6-2). It teaches a variety of skills, and the children will really enjoy making it and playing with it.

Skills to Teach

Teach children 2 years old and up:

- To follow directions
- Eye-hand coordination
- How to draw a face
- The meaning of *in half*
- The letter *V*
- To count to 7
- To count to 6

Teach children 5 years old and up:

- Cutting skills
- How to create a puppet

Materials List

- A Styrofoam egg carton, one for every two caterpillars
- Scissors
- Pipe cleaners
- Permanent markers in several different colors

Directions

Cut the lid from the egg carton with the scissors, then discard the lid. Cut the egg-cups into two strips of six cups each. Children 5 years old and up can do this cutting themselves.

Give the children an egg carton strip and seven pipe cleaners. Say to the younger children, "Here are some pipe cleaners. Count them and see how many you have." Count out loud with them: "One . . . two . . . three . . . four . . . five . . . six . . . seven." Then ask, "How many pipe cleaners do you have? That's right! *Seven*!"

Help them push the end of a pipe cleaner through one side of an eggcup, across it, and then through the other side. They can bend down both ends of the pipe cleaner to make two legs. Repeat with each eggcup until the caterpillar has 12 legs.

Children 4 years old and younger may have trouble pushing the pipe cleaner through the Styrofoam. To make it easier, poke two small holes on each side of the eggcup with a sharp object, such as a pencil. Then the child can thread the pipe cleaners through the holes; it's very good practice in eye-hand coordination.

6-2 The Egg Carton Caterpillar

There is one pipe cleaner left. Tell them to bend it in *half* so that it looks like the letter *V*. This pipe cleaner is the antennae.

Turn the caterpillar upside down. Help them push the two ends of the pipe cleaner through the top of the caterpillar's head. Turn the caterpillar back over and pull the pipe cleaners up gently as far as they will go. Fold the ends down about 1/8 inch to make them a little thicker.

Give the children permanent markers to draw big round eyes and a mouth on their creatures. Caterpillars do not have noses, but most children insist on giving them one anyway.

The markers can be used to make stripes and dots on the caterpillar's body. Ask your children how many humps their caterpillars have, including its head. Count the humps together out loud. Then ask, "How many humps does it have? That's right. *Six* humps!"

CLOTHESPIN DOLL

This wonderful old-fashioned doll leaves lots of room for a child to pretend and create. Children who are too young to cut cloth and tie yarn won't be able to make these dolls, but they do like to play with them if someone makes it for them (FIG. 6-3).

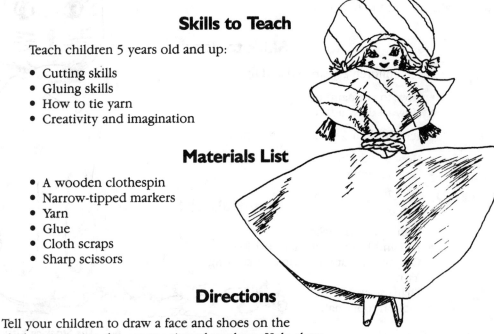

Skills to Teach

Teach children 5 years old and up:

- Cutting skills
- Gluing skills
- How to tie yarn
- Creativity and imagination

Materials List

- A wooden clothespin
- Narrow-tipped markers
- Yarn
- Glue
- Cloth scraps
- Sharp scissors

Directions

Tell your children to draw a face and shoes on the clothespin, using the narrow-tipped markers. Help them cut eight 3-inch pieces of yarn and glue them onto the doll's head for hair. They can draw hair with a marker to make a boy doll.

6-3 The Clothespin Doll

Tie the yarn together at the end with another piece of yarn to make two ponytails. Trim the ends and press the hair close to the head.

Help your children cut a 3-inch circle of cloth. They can measure it with a ruler or they can draw a circle, using a coffee cup as a pattern. Cut a 1/2-inch slit in the center of the circle. Slip it over the doll's feet and adjust it around the neck to make a shirt.

Cut three pieces of yarn 5 inches long. Tie them around the neck, under the shirt. Tie the yarn together at the ends with another piece of yarn. Trim to make wrists and hands.

Help your children cut a 4-inch circle of cloth. They can cut a 1/2-inch slit in the center of it and slip it over the doll's feet for a skirt.

They can make the clothes form-fitting around the waist by wrapping yarn three times around like a belt, then tying.

Make a hat by cutting a 1 1/2-inch circle of cloth. Cut a 1/2-inch slit in it. Slip it onto the head and adjust the brim up or down.

Your children can make a large wardrobe for their dolls by using cloth scraps. They can add to their clothespin family as long as they want, and can even make them a shoebox house.

STOCKING KITTY

A good way to use a sock that has lost a mate is by making a Stocking Kitty. Big socks make big kitties; little socks make little kitties (FIG. 6-4).

Skills to Teach

Teach children 2 years old and up:

- How to stuff and tie
- How to draw a face

Teach children 5 years old and up:

- How to tie a bow
- How to braid

Materials List

- Light-colored socks
- Red and black permanent markers
- Old nylons cut into strips for stuffing
- Yarn
- Sharp scissors
- Ribbon (optional)

6-4 The Stocking Kitty

Directions

Help each child stuff the entire foot of a sock with old nylons cut into strips.

Tie yarn one-quarter of the way down the stuffed section pulling the yarn tightly to form a head. Children 5 years old and up can do this step with very little help. Younger children will need you to do it for them.

The child should pull up two corners, one on each side of the head. They should tie these corners tightly with yarn to form ears.

Next they should tie yarn tightly at the bottom of the stuffing to form the body and keep the stuffing in place.

Help each child cut the sock top into three equal sections. These sections must be braided to form a tail. Tie the end of the braid with more yarn. Children as young as 5 years old can be taught to braid.

Now each child should draw a face on the Stocking Kitty with the black and red permanent markers. He can draw large front legs on the body as shown in FIG. 6-4. Color the fronts of the ears red.

If you wish, tie a ribbon around the Stocking Kitty's neck. Children 5 years old and up should be able to tie the bow themselves. If they can't, this is a good time to learn.

MAKING PASTE FOR CUT-AND-PASTE PAGES

White glue works so well that people don't bother anymore with homemade paste, but it's nice for the children to see that everything doesn't need to be bought in a store. Flour-water paste has been around for ages, and best of all, it's cheap.

This paste is best when made up fresh. It will keep for three days before spoiling.

Skills to Teach

Teach children 2 years old and up:

- Cutting skills
- Gluing skills
- How to write his or her first and last name

Materials List

- 1 cup cold water
- 2 tablespoons flour
- A jar with a tight-fitting lid
- A cooking pot and a wooden spoon
- A sheet of plain paper
- Old magazines with lots of pictures
- Scissors

Directions

Measure the water and flour into the jar, closing the lid tightly. Shake it vigorously until it is smooth and no lumps remain. Pour it into the cooking pot.

Cook on high heat, stirring constantly with the wooden spoon, until the mixture comes to a boil. Reduce heat and boil 1 minute. Remove the paste from the heat and pour it onto a large flat plate to let it cool quickly. Children can use popsicle sticks to spread the paste, or they can use their fingers.

Give each child a sheet of plain paper, old magazines to cut up, and a pair of scissors. Let them cut out any pictures or scraps they like and paste them on the paper. When they tire of this activity, help each child write his or her first and last names on the front of the paper. Make sure they hold their pencils correctly and use uppercase and lowercase letters.

PAPER PLATE FISH

The eyes of this hanging fish are made from the narrow lids of nonaerosol hair spray. They make the fish swing and sway (FIG. 6-5).

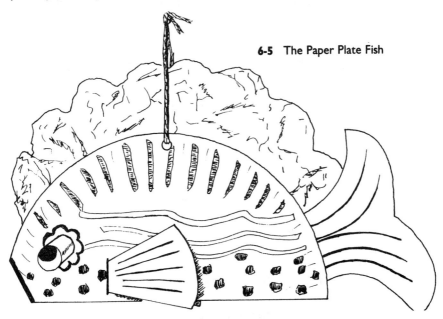

6-5 The Paper Plate Fish

Skills to Teach

Teach children 2 years old and up:

- Drawing and coloring skills
- The meaning of *insert*, *crumple*, and *between*
- How to fold something *in half*

Teach children 4 years old and up:

- Cutting and gluing skills

Materials List

- 9-inch white paper plate
- Orange construction paper
- Tissue wrapping paper, 8 × 10 inch, any color
- Two narrow lids from nonaerosol hair spray, or two milk lids
- Scissors

- Glue
- Water-base markers
- Paper punch
- String

Directions

Help your child fold the paper plate *in half*. He can decorate it by adding stripes and spots with markers.

Use the pattern in FIG. 6-6 to trace two fins and a tail onto orange construction paper. Cut these out for the younger child. Encourage children 4 years old and up to cut their own. The child can draw lines on these.

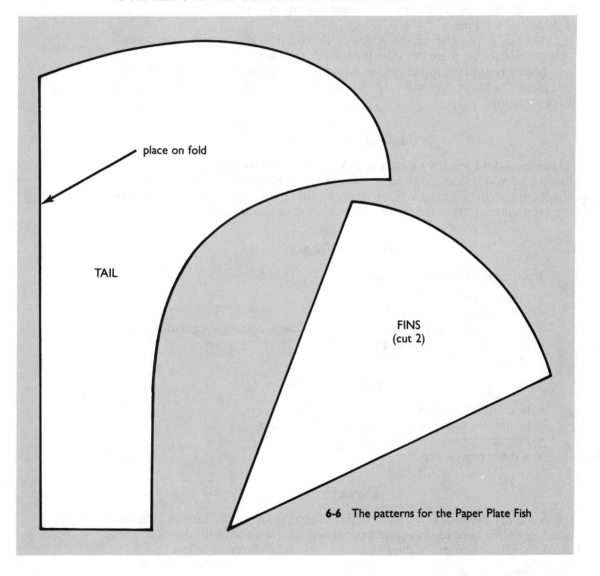

place on fold

TAIL

FINS
(cut 2)

6-6 The patterns for the Paper Plate Fish

Cut a 1-inch vertical slit on each side of the plate, about 3½ inches from the edge, so the fins can be inserted. Tell your child to *insert* the pointed tip of a fin in each slit. Help him glue the tip inside the plate so that the fins stick out.

Next, the child should *insert* the end of the tail between the plate edges, and glue it in place. He can *crumple* a piece of tissue wrapping paper and stuff it into the fish. Allow 3 inches to stick out of the plate to create a top fin. Help him glue the edges of the plate together. Then he can trim the top edge of the tissue paper in wavy lines to make a fin about 2 inches tall.

Tell him to snip off the folded tip of the plate nearest the fins. This is the fish mouth. He should add glue so the plate is closed all around its edges. Draw a line on the edge of the mouth.

Make two construction paper circles for eyes by tracing around a hair spray lid or a milk lid. The child can use a marker to draw eyeballs on these circles. Glue a circle on each lid.

Tell him to put glue on the edges of the two lids, and to press one on each side of the fish. Let them dry until they won't slide off.

Make a hole in the top of the fish with a paper punch. Insert a string and tie it in a loop. The heavy eyes make the fish jump around when you swing him gently back and forth.

LACE-A-SHAPE

The more a child actually touches and works with the five basic shapes, the more familiar he will become with them. Lace-A-Shape offers a chance to explore the shapes in a physical way, that is, by lacing around them. It encourages children to read the name of the shape and to practice eye-hand coordination (FIG. 6-7).

Skills to Teach

Teach children 2 years old and up:

- Lacing skills
- Eye-hand coordination
- The five basic shapes: *circle, square, triangle, rectangle,* and *diamond*
- How to read the names of the shapes

Materials List

- Five Styrofoam meat trays
- Permanent markers in several colors and a ruler
- Five shoelaces
- A sharp pen or pencil

Directions

Wash and dry the meat trays. Use a ruler and something round, such as a drinking glass or coffee cup, to draw one basic shape on each tray with the permanent markers. Print the name of the shape under it, using lowercase letters.

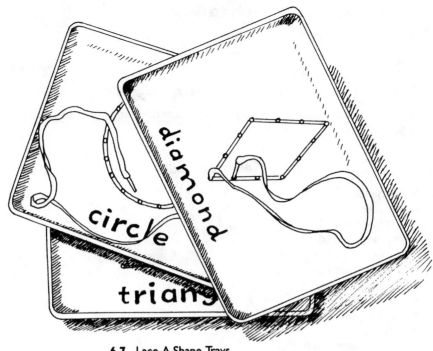

6-7 Lace-A-Shape Trays

Punch holes with a sharp pen or pencil at 1-inch intervals to outline the shapes. Tie a knot in one end of the shoelaces and string a lace through each tray.

Put the finished trays in a place where the children can work on them easily. A soft throw rug makes a nice work area. As they pick one up, teach the names of the shapes by commenting, "I see that you're lacing a round *circle*. What shape is that? Yes, a *circle*." You could also say, "You're doing a good job lacing the *diamond* shape. Can you read me the word on the card? That's right; it says, '*diamond*.'"

woolie-pullie

The circle shape is easy for children to learn. Play this game along with the Napkin Game at lunchtime. Hold up an empty lunch plate and say, "This is a circle. Liz, what shape is it?"

Liz answers, "A circle."

"That's right. You get a circle plate." Hand Liz her plate and repeat with the next child. The Napkin Game can be found in Chapter 8.

HARDTACK COOKIES

This project is not only delicious, it is also useful in teaching children how to measure.

Skills to Teach

Teach children 2 years old and up:

- To count to 4
- How to measure and stir
- The meaning of *largest*, *smallest*, *larger*, and *smaller*

Teach children 4 years old and up the differences among 1 cup, $1/2$ cup, $1/3$ cup, and $1/4$ cup.

Materials List

- A large bowl
- A wooden spoon
- A rubber spatula
- Vegetable cooking spray
- 12-×-15-inch jelly roll pan
- 2 cups quick-cooking oatmeal
- $1/2$ cup cornmeal
- $1/2$ cup oil
- $1/2$ cup honey
- $1^{1}/3$ cups flour
- $1/4$ cup brown sugar
- $1/4$ cup water
- 1 teaspoon salt

Directions

Line up four measuring cups where the children can see them: 1 cup, $1/2$ cup, $1/3$ cup, and $1/4$ cup. Help them count the cups out loud. Tell them that they will be using all four of the cups to make the Hardtack Cookies. Encourage them to pick up and examine the four cups. Ask them which cup is the *largest* and holds the most (1 cup). Which cup is the *smallest* and holds the least? ($1/4$ cup). Which cup is *larger*, $1/2$ or $1/3$ cup? ($1/2$ cup). Which of these cups is smaller? ($1/3$).

Help the children measure the oatmeal, cornmeal, oil, honey, flour, brown sugar, water, and salt into the large bowl. Let them take turns stirring the dough until it is well mixed.

Spray the jelly roll pan with vegetable cooking spray. The children can use the rubber spatula to spread and press the dough evenly until it covers the bottom of the pan.

Bake at 325°F for 30 minutes. Cut into 2-inch squares with a knife while hot and let the Hardtack Cookies cool in the pan.

This recipe makes 40 cookies. They can be frozen, or you can store them in an airtight container.

MAKING BUTTER

The old-fashioned art of making butter is easy, and the result is delicious (FIG. 6-8).

Skills to Teach

Teach children 2 years old and up:

- Where butter comes from and how it is made
- How to work together and take turns
- How to spread with a knife

Materials List

- 1/2 pint pure whipping cream (nothing added to it)
- A jar with a tight-fitting lid
- Table knives
- Crackers

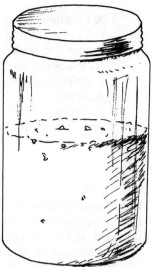

Directions

Cold whipping cream will not turn into butter, so let it sit out at room temperature for about an hour. Then pour it into a jar and close the lid tightly.

6-8 Making Butter

The children can take turns shaking the jar as hard as they can. After a few minutes the cream will become grainy-looking as the butterfat starts clumping together.

As the children continue to shake it, the butter will suddenly form as a lump, leaving the watery "buttermilk" behind.

Put the entire jar into the refrigerator until the butter becomes firm. Drain off the buttermilk, and see if anyone is brave enough to taste it. If you wish, you can instead carefully drain the buttermilk from the soft butter, putting the butter in a shallow bowl.

Give each child a table knife and a few crackers. They can spread the butter for a tasty snack.

MAKING PEANUT BUTTER

It takes a while to shell all the peanuts needed for this recipe. In the meantime the children learn a valuable lesson in cooperation. It would take much longer if one person had to shell the peanuts alone! It also teaches them why parents don't make homemade peanut butter all the time; it's so much faster to buy it at the store.

Skills to Teach

Teach children 2 years old and up:

- How peanut butter is made
- How to measure ingredients
- How to spread with a knife

Materials List

- A 12-ounce bag of roasted peanuts in the shell
  (1³/₄ cups shelled peanuts)
- 1 teaspoon sugar
- ¹/₄ teaspoon salt
- 3 tablespoons vegetable oil
- A blender
- Rubber spatula
- A table knife for each child
- Crackers

Directions

Help the children shell the peanuts and remove the brown, paper-thin membrane. Even 2-year-olds can help if you crack the shell for them.

Pour all the peanuts in a blender container. Run the blender on HIGH until the peanuts are ground into tiny bits. Stir with a rubber spatula if necessary.

Help the children measure and add 1 teaspoon sugar, ¹/₄ teaspoon salt, and 3 tablespoons vegetable oil to the ground peanuts.

Run the blender on HIGH again, stirring when necessary, until the peanut butter is thick and smooth. Scrape it into a bowl.

Put the bowl on the table where everyone can reach it. Give each child a table knife and crackers and let them spread their own homemade peanut butter.

Store the rest in a covered container in the refrigerator. This recipe yields 1 cup.

EATING SHAPES

Triangle, rectangle, square: which shall I be? Put me on a circle and then eat me!

Skills to Teach

Teach children 2 years old and up:

- The *triangle, rectangle, square,* and *circle* shapes
- How to make a sandwich, involving small motor skills and learning to follow directions

Materials List

- Two slices of bread
- Peanut butter
- Jelly
- A table knife for spreading (Plastic knives are easy for little hands to use.)
- A paper plate
- A sharp knife for an adult to use

Directions

Give your child the bread, peanut butter, and jelly. Show him how to spread peanut butter on one slice and jelly on the other slice. Then he can put the two together.

An adult can cut the sandwich into two *triangles*, two *rectangles*, or four small *squares*. Say to the child, "Look! Your sandwich has turned into *rectangles* (or whatever you cut)." "What shape is this? That's right! It's a *rectangle*!"

"Now I need a *circle* to put it on." Pick up the paper plate and put the sandwich on it. Say, "Here's a *circle*. Now you can eat your *rectangle* on a *circle*." This sounds simple, but it is a very effective way to teach shapes to a very young child.

July

July takes the children out-of-doors to collect things of nature for Masking Tape Nature Walk and Crayon Leaf Prints. They bring them home to make works of art and to increase their language skills at the same time.

Teach When You Travel

When traveling with young children, point out words to read. STOP signs are excellent to start with. Then begin reading other words along the road.

Sing nursery rhymes and the alphabet song out loud as you drive. If no one wants to chime in, pretend you enjoy singing them to yourself. You will look like you are having so much fun that soon the children will join you. If you don't know the tune, make one up. They will never know the difference. Caution: Do not sing finger game songs while driving. "One Little, Two Little, Three Little Indians" can be hazardous by the time you get to "Ten Little Indian Boys."

Craft-Training Skills to Learn

Children should be able to follow a teacher's directions when they enter school. July crafts teach the children what the teacher means by the words *large*, *small*, *longest*, *shortest*, *in between*, *in the middle*, *pleat*, *fringe*, and *assemble*. They learn that if they follow directions and do steps 1, 2, and 3 as they are told, the end result will be a nice project that they can keep or eat, whichever is appropriate.

Craft-training skills to practice in July include:

- How to use descriptive words
- The shapes and how to read their names
- Learning the names of colors
- Counting
- Learning how many make a dozen
- Drawing, cutting, gluing, coloring, and writing skills

MASKING TAPE NATURE WALK

The Masking Tape Nature Walk is a good way to start teaching your children about the world of nature. They will also have a memento of this time you shared.

Skills to Teach

Teach children 2 years old and up:

- An awareness of the small things around them
- The beauty of nature
- How to describe things
- Counting skills
- Gluing skills
- How to write numbers
- How to write his or her own name

Materials List

- A roll of masking tape—the wider, the better
- A sheet of construction paper for each child
- Glue
- Crayons or a pencil

Directions

Use the masking tape to make a loose bracelet around each child's wrist. Make sure the sticky part of the tape is facing *outward*, not against the skin.

Go for a walk in a park, field, or forest preserve—wherever there are trees, grass, and rocks.

Encourage your children to look for small things that can be stuck to the masking tape bracelet. They might include a pretty pebble, a feather, a tiny pinecone, an acorn, a fuzzy grass, a wild flower, and a small leaf.

As you walk along and they select their treasures, comment on each one by naming and describing it. You might say, "What a lovely pebble. It's so smooth and brown," Or, "Did you find a white feather? It will stick to your bracelet, I bet." Or, "That's such a tiny brown pinecone! I wonder which tree it fell from." In this way you will be teaching them how to describe things in terms of color, size, texture, and place of origin.

Encourage them to take only one of each thing they find, or they may cover their bracelet with leaves and be finished very quickly. That's not the idea of the Nature Walk.

When the bracelet is full, carefully remove it from their wrists until you return home. Once home they can make a collage from their collections by gluing them onto the sheet of construction paper.

Ask them to count the number of items they have collected. Count them out loud with each child. Then ask, "How many things did you collect?" He should tell you the number. Help him write this number on the front of his collage.

Now they should print their name on the collage, using uppercase and lower-case letters. Make sure they hold their pencil or crayon correctly for writing.

If they are interested, they can print the name of each object next to it, with your help.

KITCHEN COLLAGE

Strong tea makes a golden nontoxic wood stain. The children add rows of spices to create a fragrant design. This craft makes a lovely gift for Mother or a favorite teacher. It takes three days to complete (FIG. 7-1).

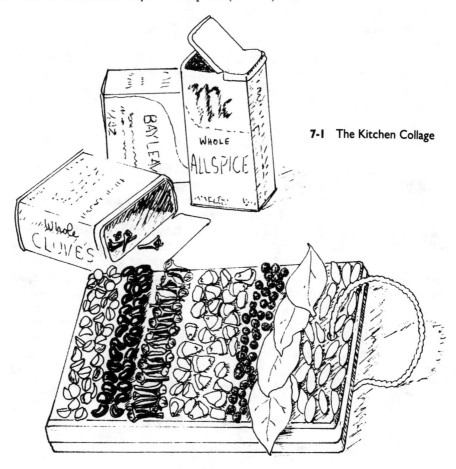

7-1 The Kitchen Collage

Skills to Teach

Teach children 4 years old and up:

- How to use sandpaper
- How to make a gift from wood
- How to stain wood
- Patience in completing a project

Materials List

A note about the wood for this craft: *1 × 3 Finished Fir* is sold in builder's supply stores in lengths of 6 feet and longer. It is inexpensive (1989 price from Home Depot is $2.19) and can be cut into 4¹/₂-inch lengths for this project. A 6-foot board makes 16 Kitchen Collages at 14¢ each. Drill a hole in the top of each Collage so it can be hung, or staple a loop of ribbon on the back of the finished craft with a staple gun.

- A 4¹/₂-inch piece of 1 × 3 Finished Fir
- Sandpaper
- Two tea bags
- 1 cup water in a pot
- Glue
- Kitchen seeds and spices such as dried seeds from a honeydew melon, whole bay leaves, whole allspice, popcorn, whole cloves, black beans, and split peas.
- ³/₈-inch ribbon, any color

Directions

Give your child the wood and sandpaper. Finished Fir does not need a lot of sanding, which makes it nice for this craft.

While the child is sanding the wood, boil the two tea bags in a cup of water for three minutes. Leave the tea bags in the water and let it cool.

When the wood is smooth, the child can put it in the tea and can use the tea bags like a sponge to pat the tea all over the wood. Let the wood dry overnight.

The next day give the child a small squirt bottle of glue, the wood, and kitchen seeds and spices. He should squirt a row of glue on the wood, press spices into it, then add another row of glue and spices until the Kitchen Collage is full of rows. Let it dry overnight.

On the third day the child can cut a ribbon long enough to fit around the outside edge of the Collage. He should squirt a very thin line of glue around the edge of the wood and press the ribbon onto it.

An adult can finish the Kitchen Collage by threading a ribbon through the hole drilled in it or by stapling a ribbon loop on the back with a staple gun.

EGG CARTON FLOWERS

Egg carton flowers are delightful as a teaching tool and a decoration (FIG. 7-2).

Skills to Teach

Teach children 2 years old and up:

- To count to *12*
- How many make a *dozen*

- How to put things together
- The meaning of *in the middle*

Teach children 4 years old and up cutting skills.

Materials List

- Styrofoam egg cartons
- Construction paper, any colors
- 12 pipe cleaners
- Scissors

Directions

For each child, cut the lid off the egg carton and discard it. Cut the carton into 12 separate eggcups. Snip the sides of each cup so that it has four petals. You can make the petals pointed by snipping out small triangles from each cup, or you can make them rounded by cutting more carefully. Older children with pretty good cutting skills (ages 8 years old and up) can make these cups themselves.

Use the patterns in FIGS. 7-3 and 7-4 to trace 12 construction paper flowers. A faster way to make the flowers is to draw four circles on a sheet of paper, using a small cereal bowl or a large cup. Cut them out. Fold two of the circles together into fourths, then cut a ruffled or rounded shape out of this quarter. Unfold, and you will have two paper flowers.

7-2 Egg Carton Flowers

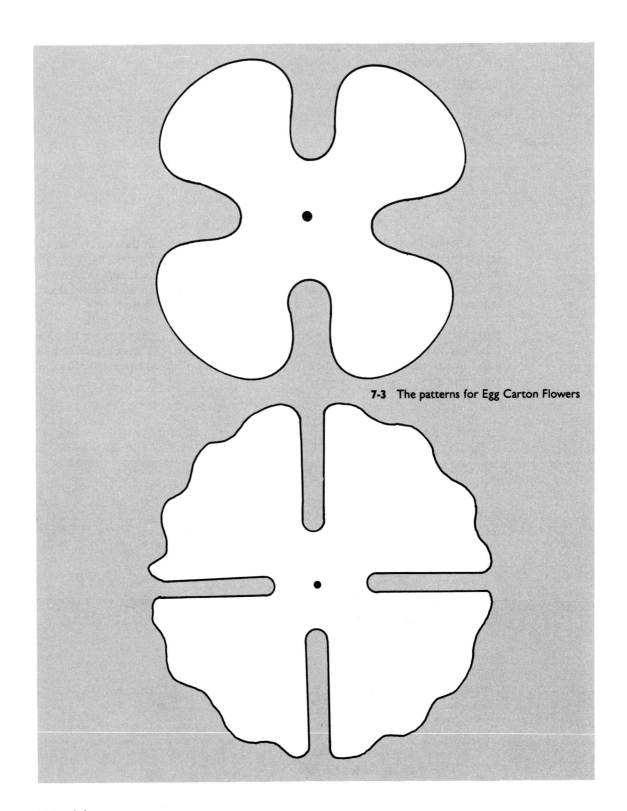

7-3 The patterns for Egg Carton Flowers

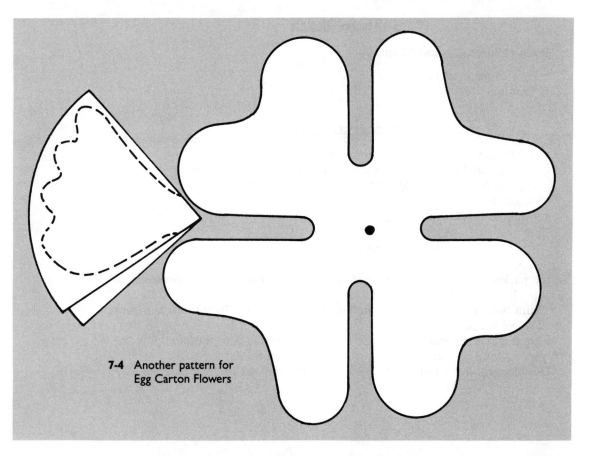

7-4 Another pattern for Egg Carton Flowers

Tell the children that there are enough eggcups to make a *dozen* flowers. Ask, "How many make a *dozen*? Let's count the eggcups and find out." Count the eggcups out loud, together with the children. "One, two, three," and so on to 12. Then ask again, "How many make a *dozen*? *Twelve*! There are *twelve* eggcups in a *dozen*."

Show the children how to use the sharp pipe cleaner to poke a hole *in the middle* of a paper flower, then *in the middle* of an eggcup.

Bend the very tip of the pipe cleaner over on the inside of the cup, to hold it in place. Make a second little bend under the paper flower to keep it from sliding down the pipe cleaner.

A 2-year-old can assemble his or her own flowers if you poke a tiny hole in the middle of the eggcups and in the paper flowers first. He will still get lots of practice in eye-hand coordination and assembly skills by putting the flowers together himself.

TISSUE PAPER FLOWERS

These flowers can be put on packages, or used as a decoration for a table or pillow. They make nice gifts for a teacher, a scout leader, or for someone who is sick (FIG. 7-7).

Skills to Teach

Teach children 2 years old and up:

- How to pleat paper
- To follow directions

Materials List

- A 20-sheet package of tissue wrapping paper, 1 foot, 6 inches × 2 feet, 2 inches (One package will give you enough tissue for 6 flowers)
- Scissors
- 6 rubber bands

Directions

Cut the package of tissue paper in half across the middle without opening it or unfolding it.

Count out six to eight sheets of tissue for each flower. Treat them as if they were a single sheet.

Help the children start at the narrow end of the tissue paper and fold it in 1/2-inch pleats. Make sure they press down hard to crease the folded edges.

Double a rubber band tightly around the middle of the pleated tissue (FIG. 7-5).

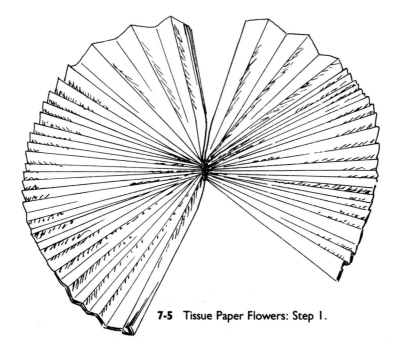

7-5 Tissue Paper Flowers: Step 1.

Show the children how to carefully separate one thin sheet of tissue paper. Tug at it gently until it is sticking up in the air. Continue pulling it upward completely around the flower (FIG. 7-6).

7-6 Tissue Paper Flowers: Step 2.

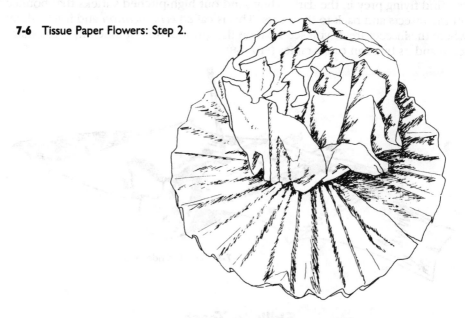

Each child should separate a second sheet of tissue paper and pull it upward all the way around. They should continue separating and pulling up the layers of tissue paper until all the layers are pulled up.

Pull the bottom layer downward all the way around to give each flower a fluffy look (FIG. 7-7).

7-7 Tissue Paper Flowers: Step 3.

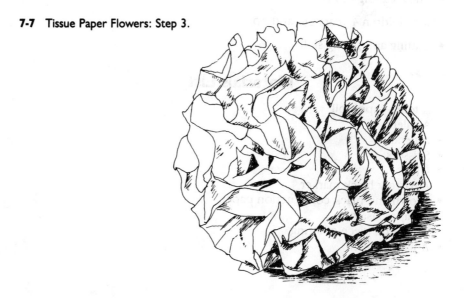

CYLINDER BAT

Bats are helpful animals because they eat insects. They have very big ears so they can find flying prey in the dark. They send out high-pitched shrieks that bounce off the insects and back to their ears. This is called *echolocation* and it tells them where the insects are. If you see a bat on the ground, do not touch it. It has sharp teeth and its bite can cause rabies (FIG. 7-8).

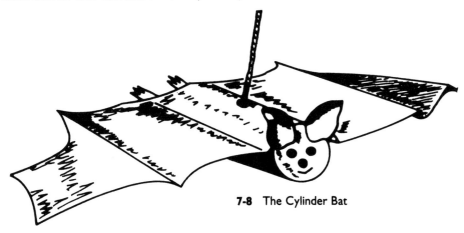

7-8 The Cylinder Bat

Skills to Teach

Teach children 3 years old and up:

- The *rectangle, circle,* and *cylinder* shapes
- The meaning of *nocturnal, mammals,* and *echolocation*
- The meaning of *insect*

Teach children 4 years old and up:

- Cutting and gluing skills

Materials List

- A toilet-paper roll
- A ruler
- A pencil
- Scissors
- Glue
- A narrow black marker
- Brown and black construction paper
- A paper fastener
- A 24-inch piece of string
- A paper punch

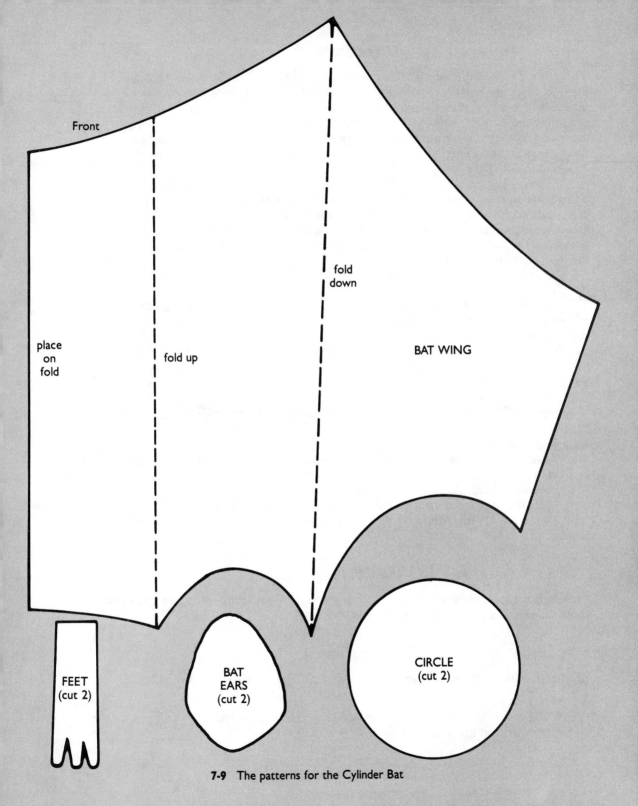

Front

place
on
fold

fold up

fold
down

BAT WING

FEET
(cut 2)

BAT
EARS
(cut 2)

CIRCLE
(cut 2)

7-9 The patterns for the Cylinder Bat

Directions

If possible, find a picture of a real bat to show to the children. Explain that bats are the only flying *mammals*, or animals that feed milk to their babies. They are *nocturnal*, which means they sleep during the day and wake up at night. Tell the children how the bats use *echolocation* to catch their dinner. Explain to them why they have little eyes but need big ears; they don't *see* the insects, but must *hear* them to catch them. This is a good time to reinforce the idea that *insects* have six legs, and usually have two pairs of wings.

To make each bat, use the pencil and ruler to draw a rectangle $4^1/2 \times 6$ inches on brown construction paper. Use the patterns in FIG. 7-9 to trace two circles, two ears, and two feet on brown paper. To make the wings, fold brown paper in half crosswise. Again use the pattern in FIG. 7-9 to trace wings onto the paper, with the flat side of the pattern placed on the fold. Cut through both papers, but do not cut the fold. Open the wings.

Cut out all pieces for the younger child. Encourage children 4 years old and up to cut their own.

Instruct the children as follows: "Spread glue on the brown *rectangle*. Wrap the *rectangle* around the *cylinder*, covering it completely. This *cylinder* is the bat's body.

"Glue the wings to the body. *Insert* a paper fastener through the back of the bat. (Use a sharp pencil to punch a hole for the paper fastener to go through.) Tie a piece of string to the fastener. Spread out the tabs of the fastener inside the cylinder to hold the string in place.

"Make the face of the bat from a brown *circle*. Glue on two black eyes and a black nose made with the paper punch. Draw a *V* mouth. Fold the ears in half the long way. Open them and glue them above the eyes.

"Spread glue on each end of the cylinder with your finger. Gently place the face on the front end of the bat. Press the other *circle* on the other end of the bat. If you press too hard, the bat will eat his circles!

"Glue the feet under each side of the wing. The place is marked on the pattern. Let the bat dry for awhile. Then fly him around by the string so he can catch insects."

TWO-PIECE PUZZLES

This craft is especially useful for very young children. Older children can make these puzzles as a gift for younger friends (FIG. 7-10).

Skills to Teach

Teach children 2 years old and up:

- How to put puzzles together
- The *circle, square, diamond, rectangle,* and *triangle* shapes
- How to read the names of the shapes

Materials List

- Five Styrofoam meat trays
- A permanent marker
- A razor blade for you to use
- A ruler

Directions

Wash and dry the meat trays. With a permanent marker, draw one large shape on each tray. You might use a cereal bowl or a coffee cup to draw a circle. Use the ruler to draw a square, diamond, rectangle, and triangle on the other four trays.

Use the razor blade to carefully cut the shape out of the tray, so the tray and the shape stay intact. Print the name of each shape on the tray and on the cutout shape with the marker.

Show your children how to put the shapes back in their holes. They can learn to match and read the names of the shapes at the same time.

You can teach them the names of the five shapes by saying, "Here is a tray that says *'Diamond.'* Which is the *diamond* shape? Can you put it in the puzzle?" Show them the diamond shape matches the hole in the diamond tray. Also point out that it is the same as the word 'Diamond' printed on the shape. Go through this process very quickly to keep their attention.

Repeat this method to teach a child the other shapes. Then try this game: Give him the five shapes and spread the five trays out in front of him. Point to the circle tray. Say "This word says *'Circle'*. Do you have a *circle* in your hand? Does it fit in the tray? What does the word say on your shape? It says *'Circle.'*"

Repeat this game with the remaining trays and shapes.

7-10 Two-Piece Puzzles

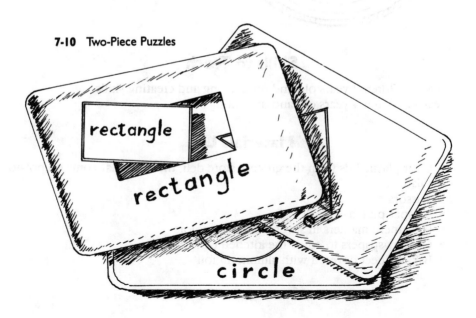

DELI LID NECKLACE

We had fun experimenting with lots of different disposable plastic lids by melting them in the oven. The best ones for crafts are the deli lids (FIG. 7-11).

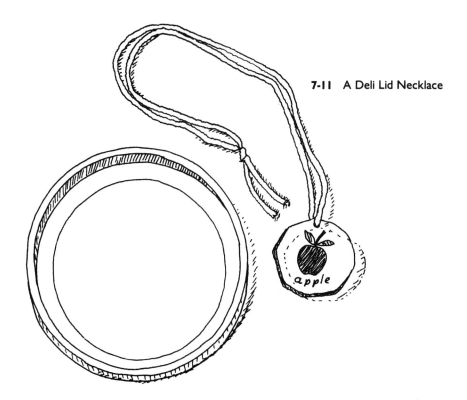

7-11 A Deli Lid Necklace

Skills to Teach

Teach children 2 years old and up drawing and creating skills.
Teach children 4 years old and up cutting skills.

Materials List

- Clear plastic lids from the grocery store deli, the kind that come on potato salad.
- Scissors
- A paper punch
- Permanent markers in several different colors
- Old newspapers to cover the kitchen table
- Baking sheet covered with aluminum foil
- Yarn

Directions

Preheat the oven to 325 °F, and spread newspapers on the kitchen table.

Give the children the deli lids, scissors, and markers. Tell them to cut the rim from the deli lid, leaving a large circle. Encourage children 4 years old and up to do the cutting themselves. Younger children will need help from you.

They can decorate the circle with markers by making designs, writing their names, or drawing pictures.

Use the paper punch to make a hole in the circle. Place the circles on a baking sheet covered with aluminum foil.

Bake at 325 °F for 4 minutes. The circle will curl and shrink while baking, and will be fairly flat when finished.

Remove the lids from the oven, peeling them off the aluminum foil if necessary, and let them cool. The children can thread yarn through the hole to make a necklace.

CHEESE STRAWS

Cheese straws are a delicious treat your children will enjoy making and eating.

Skills to Teach

Teach children 2 years old and up:

- To sit still, listen, and follow directions
- How to measure, stir, roll, and bake

Materials List

- A large bowl
- A pastry blender or two table knives
- A breadboard and rolling pin
- A baking sheet
- A pizza cutter
- $2^1/2$ cups flour
- 1 teaspoon salt
- $1^1/2$ cups grated cheddar cheese
- $2/3$ cup vegetable shortening
- $1/2$ cup cold water

Directions

Help the children measure the flour, salt, grated cheese, and shortening into a large bowl. They can take turns using the pastry blender to cut the shortening and cheese into small bits the size of rice grains, or use two table knives in a cutting motion.

Help them measure the cold water and add it to the flour mixture. Stir until all the flour is moistened. Then the children can press the dough together by hand until it forms a smooth ball.

Divide the dough among the children. They can take turns rolling their dough very thin on the breadboard. Lay the rolled dough on an ungreased baking sheet. Help the children use the pizza cutter to cut it into narrow strips.

Bake in a preheated oven at 425 °F for 5 to 8 minutes, until the dough turns a golden brown. Remove the Cheese Straws from the pan with a wide spatula. Break apart when cool, and store in an airtight container.

PEANUT BUTTER/POPCORN BALLS

The children can help you make another tasty treat, the Peanut Butter/Popcorn Balls.

Materials List

- 8 cups popped corn in a large bowl or pan
- A 1-quart saucepan and a wooden spoon
- 1/2 cup corn syrup
- 1/4 cup sugar
- 1/2 cup peanut butter
- Butter or margarine

Directions

Measure the corn syrup and sugar into the saucepan. Cook over medium heat, stirring constantly, until the mixture comes to a boil and the sugar is completely dissolved.

Remove the pan from the heat and stir in the peanut butter until smooth. Pour this mixture over the popped corn. Stir it until the corn is coated.

Give each child a small piece of butter or margarine. Tell them to coat their hands with it, and then shape the popcorn into balls the size of a baseball. They should squeeze the ball to make it stick together.

The yield is about 12 balls.

PEANUT BUTTER CRUMBLES

These treats are called Crumbles because they crumble when you eat them.

Skills to Teach

Teach children 2 years old and up:

- To sit still, listen, and follow directions
- Descriptive words such as *sticky, crisp, firmly,* and *delicious*
- How to measure and stir
- To count to *9*

Materials List

- A 12-ounce package butterscotch chips
- 1 cup peanut butter
- 9 cups crispy rice cereal
- A large bowl and a wooden spoon
- A 10-×-15-inch jellyroll pan

Directions

Measure the butterscotch chips and the peanut butter in the top of a double boiler. Melt over boiling water, stirring until smooth.

Microwave Directions: Measure the butterscotch chips and the peanut butter into a large microwave bowl. Microwave on high for 3 minutes. Remove from the oven. Let the children stir this mixture with a wooden spoon until smooth.

Help the children measure and add 9 cups of crispy rice cereal. Count out loud with the children as they add it: "One . . . two . . . three . . . four . . . five . . . six . . . seven . . . eight . . . nine. How many cups of cereal did you add? *Nine*."

The children can take turns stirring this mixture with the wooden spoon. One child at a time, please, unless you enjoy mopping the kitchen floor.

One or two children can grease the jellyroll pan with a pastry brush, a piece of waxed paper, or their hands.

Pour the Crumbles mixture into the prepared pan. The children can butter their hands and press the mixture *firmly* into the pan. The cookies will be very *sticky* until they are refrigerated. Refrigerate for 1 hour, then cut into 48 squares.

Note how *delicious* they taste. "Aren't these *delicious, crisp* Peanut Butter Crumbles!"

August

School is approaching for older children, making it easier to interest preschoolers in alphabet crafts such as Letters in Yarn and Pretzel Alphabets. Fall crafts include pictures made of seeds and leaves that the children can gather in the garden or the park.

The Napkin Game

Lunchtime is a good time to teach shapes. The children are starving and will not get up until you feed them. They don't realize that you are going to teach them first. Do you pass out napkins for their messy mouths? Do it with the Napkin Game.

Hold up a paper napkin. Say, "This is a square. What shape is it?"

The children answer, "A square."

Fold the napkin over into a triangle. Say, "Look! Now it's a triangle. What shape is it?"

The children say, "A triangle."

Open the napkin and fold it into a rectangle. Tell them, "Look! Now it's a rectangle. What shape is it?"

The children answer, "A rectangle."

Next say, "If you can tell me the shape, you can have the napkin." Fold the napkin into a triangle or a rectangle, or leave it as a square. Then call a child by name. "Mary, what shape is this?"

Mary says, "A triangle."

Tell her, "That's right. You get a triangle." Give Mary the triangle napkin and quickly go on to the next child. Keep the game fast and short. Play it every day.

Craft-Training Skills to Learn

August crafts introduce the children to *phonics*, or the sounds the letters make in words. They can work on letters made of yarn and pretzels, and shapes made of yarn and biscuit dough.

Craft-training skills for August include:

- How to glue, cut, draw, and color
- How to read and write his or her name
- How to read and write the names of the shapes
- How to be creative with dough
- Learning how bread is made

SEED MOSAIC

A *mosaic* is a picture made of small things of different colors, arranged to form a design. When making Seed Mosaics, the seeds usually end up everywhere; so this is a good outdoor craft (FIG. 8-1).

Skills to Teach

Teach children 2 years old and up:

- Drawing skills
- How to write his or her name

Teach children 4 years old and up:

- The meaning of *mosaic*
- How to follow directions
- How to create a design with seeds

Materials List

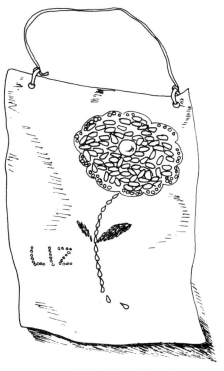

8-1   A Seed Mosaic

- Newspapers
- 12-×-9-inch sheet construction paper
- Crayons
- At least three of the following seeds, in separate bowls:
  - ~ Unpopped popcorn
  - ~ Dried pumpkin or watermelon seeds
  - ~ Dried beans
  - ~ Dried peas
  - ~ Bird seed
- White glue
- 11-×-13-inch plastic food storage bags
- Cellophane tape
- A paper punch
- Yarn

Directions

Tell the children to draw a design on the construction paper, using crayons. The design or picture should be large enough to cover most of the page. They can draw anything, and it will be beautiful when completed in seed mosaic.

Each child should write his or her name on the paper, using uppercase and lowercase letters. Make sure they hold their crayon correctly when writing and drawing.

Cover the kitchen table or a picnic table outside with newspapers. Spread glue on part of each child's picture. If the child has drawn a house, for instance, cover only the roof. Let him pour one kind of seed, such as popcorn, on the glue.

Then he can turn the picture on end, dumping the popcorn off. Some will stick to the glue on the picture. Return the rest to its bowl.

Cover another part of each child's picture with glue. If the child has drawn a scribble all over the page, follow part of the scribble with glue. Let him pour on a second kind of seed. He can then dump it off and return it to its container. Some will remain stuck to the glue, and you will see an attractive design beginning to take shape.

Continue with the rest of the picture and the remaining seeds until each child's entire tracing is covered in seeds of different kinds.

Let the design lay flat to dry overnight. The next day slip the picture into a food storage bag. Fold the end of the bag over and tape it shut to keep loose seeds from falling on the floor.

Punch two holes through each paper and plastic in the top of the picture, one on each side. Tie a piece of yarn through the holes to hang up the Seed Mosaic.

If the picture bends and cannot be hung, tape a piece of heavy cardboard 2 × 12 inches on the back, just below the holes.

TOOTHPICK PICTURE

A box of toothpicks, construction paper, and glue are all you need for these Toothpick Pictures (FIG. 8-2).

Skills to Teach

Teach children 2 years old and up:

- The color *black*
- Eye-hand coordination
- How to use imagination to "draw" with toothpicks

Materials List

- Black construction paper
- A box of toothpicks
- White glue

Directions

Give your children some toothpicks and a sheet of construction paper. Tell them to make a picture or a design by arranging the toothpicks on the *black* paper.

When they are finished, glue their toothpick picture to the paper by picking the toothpicks up one by one, applying white glue, and putting them back in their place. Children 6 years old and up can do this step themselves.

If they tell you a story about their Toothpick Picture, jot it down and glue it to the picture.

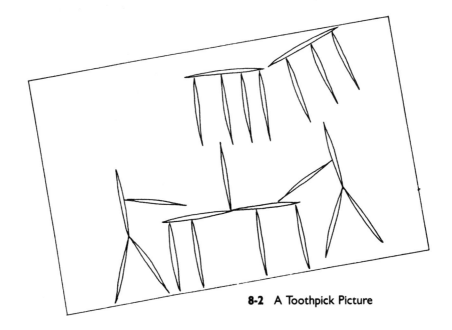

8-2 A Toothpick Picture

DONNIE DOG JUICE CAN ANIMAL

Donnie Dog says, "Bow wow wow! I'll hold your pencils. I know how!" (FIG. 8-3).

Skills to Teach

Teach children 3 years old and up:

- Following instructions
- Listening skills
- Gluing skills
- How to make a useful item from an orange-juice can

Materials List

- A 12-oz. orange-juice can
- Brown, black, white, and red construction paper
- Glue in a milk lid
- A pencil
- A ruler
- Scissors

8-3 Donnie Dog Juice Can Animal

Directions

Measure and draw a 5-×-9-inch rectangle on brown construction paper. Cut it out. Use the patterns in FIG. 8-4 to trace and cut out the following pieces: two brown ears, two brown front feet, two brown back feet, a brown tail, two small white circle eyes, two black circle eyeballs, one large white circle nose, one smaller black circle nose, a red tongue, and six whiskers cut in thin strips from black paper.

Give these pieces to the child. Then tell her the following:

"Spread glue on the brown rectangle and wrap it around the orange-juice can, covering the can completely. This is Donnie Dog's body.

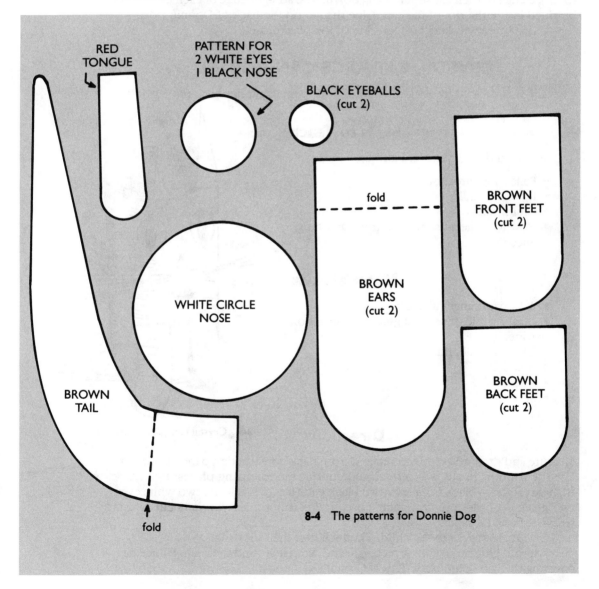

RED TONGUE

PATTERN FOR 2 WHITE EYES 1 BLACK NOSE

BLACK EYEBALLS (cut 2)

BROWN FRONT FEET (cut 2)

fold

BROWN EARS (cut 2)

WHITE CIRCLE NOSE

BROWN BACK FEET (cut 2)

BROWN TAIL

fold

8-4 The patterns for Donnie Dog

"Glue two small white circle eyes close together near the top of the can. Glue two small black circle eyeballs on the white eyes.

"Glue the large white circle nose in the middle of the can, below the eyes. Glue the black circle nose in the middle of this white circle.

"Glue the red tongue on the white circle, just below the black nose.

"Glue two long front feet on the front of the dog. The rounded edges can hang down below the can. Bend the edges up to make paws.

"Glue the two short back feet under the can, one on each side. Let them stick out so you can see them.

"Glue the ears at the top of the can, one on each side of the eyes. The rounded edge of each ear should hang down. The straight edge of each ear should be glued inside the rim of the can. Glue the tail on the back of Donnie Dog.

"Glue three whiskers on each side of the black nose."

CRYSTAL CAT JUICE CAN ANIMAL

Crystal Cat is dressed in black. She holds your pencils on her back (FIG. 8-5).

Skills to Teach

Teach children 3 years old and up:

- Following directions
- Listening skills
- Gluing skills
- How to make a useful item from an orange-juice can

Materials List

- A 12-oz. orange-juice can
- Black, white, pink, and green construction paper
- Glue in a milk lid
- A pencil
- A ruler
- Scissors

Directions

8-5 Crystal Cat Juice Can Animal

Measure and draw a 5-×-9-inch rectangle on black construction paper. Cut it out. Use the patterns in FIG. 8-6 to trace and cut out the following pieces: two black triangle ears, two black front feet, two black back feet, a black tail, two white eyes, two green eyeballs, a pink triangle nose, a pink mouth, six whiskers cut in thin strips from black paper.

Give these pieces to the child. Then tell him the following:

"Spread glue on the black rectangle and wrap it around the orange-juice can, covering the can completely. This is Crystal Cat's body.

"Glue two white eyes close together near the top of the can. Glue the two green eyeballs on the white eyes. Look at the illustration to see how the eyes should look.

"Glue the pink triangle nose in the middle of the can, below the eyes. Glue the pink mouth below the nose.

"Glue two long front feet on the front of the cat, close together. The rounded edges can hang down below the can. Bend the edges up to make paws.

"Glue the two short back feet under the can, one on each side. Let them stick out so you can see them.

"Glue the two black triangle ears inside the top of the can above the eyes. They should be close together.

"Glue the tail on the back of Crystal Cat. Glue three whiskers on each side of her nose."

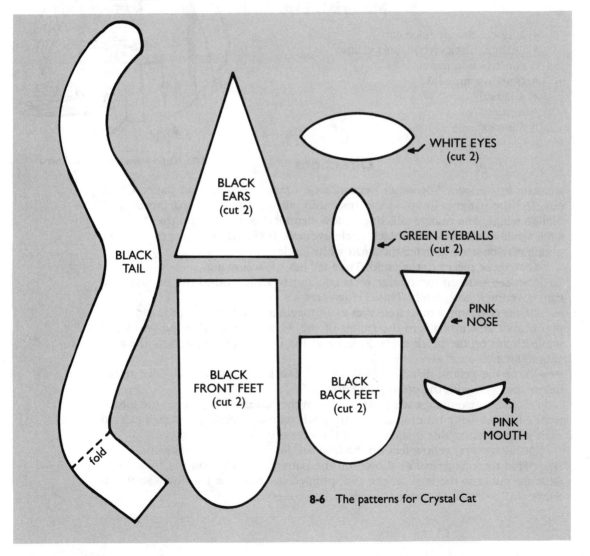

8-6 The patterns for Crystal Cat

HUGO HAWK JUICE CAN ANIMAL

Hugo Hawk has great big eyes. Fill him with pencils and pretend he flies (FIG. 8-7).

Skills to Teach

Teach children 3 years old and up:

- Following directions
- Listening skills
- Gluing skills
- How to make a useful item from an orange-juice can

Materials List

- A 12-oz. orange-juice can
- Orange, black, white, and yellow construction paper
- Glue in a milk lid
- A pencil
- A ruler
- Scissors

8-7 Hugo Hawk Juice Can Animal

Directions

Measure and draw a 5-×-9-inch rectangle on orange construction paper. Cut it out. Use the patterns in FIG. 8-8 to trace and cut out the following pieces: two orange wings, one orange tail, one yellow diamond beak, two yellow feet, two large white circle eyes, two black circle eyeballs, two small circle eyes. A paper punch may be used to make the small white circles.

Give these pieces to the child. Then tell her the following:

"Spread glue on the orange rectangle and wrap it around the orange-juice can, covering it completely. This is Hugo Hawk's body.

"Glue two large white circle eyes close together near the top of the can. Glue two black circle eyeballs in the center of the white circles. Glue the two small white circles on the black eyeballs. Look at the illustration to see how the eyes should look.

"Fold the yellow diamond beak in half. Put glue on one half. Glue it just below the eyes, with the point going down.

"Fold the two orange wings as shown on the pattern. Put glue on the folded tabs. Glue one wing on each side of the owl, with the wings pointing up. Fold each wing down so that it sticks out at the side as if Hugo is flying.

"Glue the two yellow feet on the front of the can. Bend the toes up.

"Fold the orange tail as shown on the pattern. Put glue on the folded tab. Glue the tail onto the back of the owl, pointed up. Fold the tail down so that it sticks out."

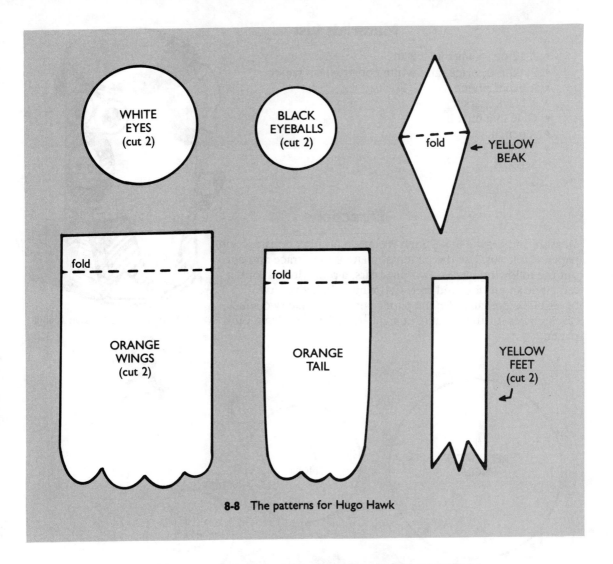

8-8 The patterns for Hugo Hawk

PUNKY PIG JUICE CAN ANIMAL

Pink Punky Pig is round and fat. He uses pencils as a hat! (FIG. 8-9).

Skills to Teach

Teach children 3 years old and up:

- Following instructions
- Listening skills
- Gluing skills
- How to make a useful item from an orange-juice can

Materials List

- A 12-oz. orange-juice can
- Pink, red, black, and white construction paper
- A paper punch
- A black marker
- Glue in a milk lid
- A pencil
- A ruler
- Scissors

Directions

Measure and draw a 5-×-9-inch rectangle on pink construction paper. Cut it out. Use the patterns in FIG. 8-10 to trace and cut out the following pieces: two pink ears, a pink circle snout, a red circle snout, four red feet, two white circle eyes, two black circle eyeballs. Use the paper punch to make two small black circles for the snout. Cut a tail 1/2 × 3 inches from pink paper.

8-9 Punky Pig Juice Can Animal

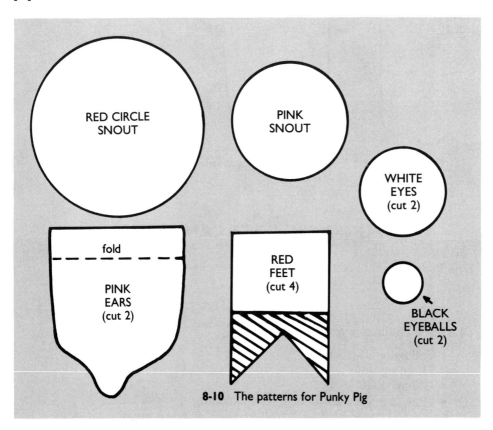

8-10 The patterns for Punky Pig

Give these to the child. Then tell him the following:

"Spread glue on the pink rectangle and wrap it around the orange-juice can, covering the can completely. This is Punky Pig's body.

"Glue two white circle eyes close together near the top of the can. Glue two black circle eyeballs on the white eyes.

"Glue the large red circle just below the eyes. Glue the pink circle snout in the middle of this red circle. Glue two black circles in the middle of the pink snout to look like snout holes. Make these with the paper punch and black paper.

"Color the hoof-end of each foot with a black marker. Glue two feet on the front of the pig, and two feet on the sides of the pig with the hooves aiming forward a little. This will make your pig look like he is sitting up.

"Fold each ear as shown on the pattern. Put glue on the tabs, and stick one ear on each side of the can, with the point going down. Look at the illustrations to see how Punky Pig should look.

"Curl the tail by wrapping it tightly around a pencil. Remove the pencil, and glue the tail on the back of the pig, near the bottom of the can."

PRETZEL ALPHABET

The Pretzel Alphabet project allows you to teach the alphabet with pretzels (FIG. 8-11).

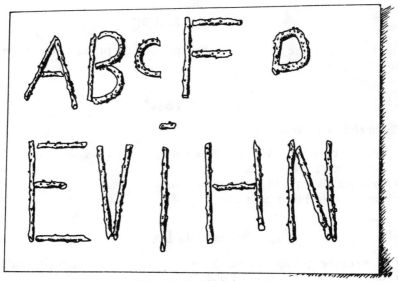

8-11 Pretzel Alphabet

Skills to Teach

Teach children of all ages:

- How to form letters of the alphabet
- How to write his or her first and last name

Materials List

- A sheet of construction paper for each child
- A pencil for each child
- A box of straight pretzel sticks
- A box of twisted pretzels
- White glue

Directions

Give each of the children a sheet of construction paper and a pencil. Help them print their first and last names on the paper. Make sure each one holds the pencil the right way. Spell the children's names out loud to them as they write the letters. "Your last name is Smith. *S−M−I−T−H*."

Put a bowl of straight pretzels and a bowl of twisted pretzels on the table where everyone can reach them. It's best to do this craft after lunch when they're not too hungry.

Show them how to make letters by putting the pretzels together on their sheet of construction paper, breaking them when needed. The children will come up with some pretty interesting combinations.

When they have finished, they can glue the letters they have made to the construction paper for display and eat the scraps.

BAKE-A-SHAPE

The five basic shapes are the basis for the Bake-A-Shape project. One shape can be taught per session.

Skills to Teach

Teach children 2 years old and up:

- The five basic shapes: *rectangle, square, circle, triangle,* and *diamond*
- How to work with dough
- To sit still, listen, and follow directions
- How to write his or her name

Materials List

- A can of refrigerator biscuits. (Plan on using three biscuits per child.)
- Melted butter and a pastry brush
- $1/4$ cup sugar mixed with 1 tablespoon cinnamon
- A baking sheet covered with aluminum foil
- Paper plates
- Markers or crayons

Directions

Give each child three refrigerator biscuits. Tell them to roll each biscuit into a long snake.

The children can take turns placing their snakes on the foil-covered baking sheet, pinching them together to form a shape, such as a *rectangle*. Then they can brush the shape with melted butter and sprinkle it with the cinnamon-sugar mixture.

Bake in a preheated oven at 475 °F for 4 or 5 minutes. While the shapes are baking, give each of the children a paper plate and markers or crayons. Tell them to turn their plates over and to print their names, using uppercase and lowercase letters, on the back of the plate. Make sure they hold the markers correctly when writing.

Carefully transfer the cooled shapes to the children's plates. Ask each child the name of the shape he has baked, or comment, "You certainly did a good job baking that *rectangle*."

Repeat this activity at another time to teach a different shape.

COFFEE CAN COOKIE JAR

Do this project one day and a cookie project the next, so each child can have his or her own cookies in a cookie jar (FIG. 8-12).

Skills to Teach

Teach children 2 years old and up:

- Drawing, coloring, and gluing skills
- How to write his or her name

Teach children 4 years old and up cutting skills.

Materials List

- A ruler and pencil
- Scissors
- A 13-ounce coffee can with a plastic lid for each child
- Construction paper
- White glue
- Cellophane tape
- White (typing) paper
- Water-based markers and crayons

8-12 A Coffee Can Cookie Jar

Directions

Using a ruler, pencil, and scissors, cut a 5¹/₂-×-12-inch strip of construction paper for each cookie jar. This strip will not fit all the way around the coffee cans, so cut a second piece of construction paper 5¹/₂ × 3¹/₂ inches for each can.

Apply the smaller piece of paper to the can first. Spread glue on it and press it onto the can just under the top metal rim. Tuck the excess paper under the can.

Apply the larger piece of paper in the same way. Tape the seams and bottom to hold the paper securely.

Children 8 years old and up can cover their cans with paper themselves. Children 6 and 7 years old can glue the paper if you measure and cut it for them. Younger children should be given the covered can to decorate.

Lay the remaining scrap of construction paper on the plastic lid. Run a pencil around the inside circle of the lid to mark the paper. Cut out this circle and glue it on the lid.

Give your children the white paper, markers, crayons, scissors, and glue. Tell them to draw and color lots of cookies of different shapes and sizes. Then they can cut them out and glue them all over their cookie jar. Each child should print his or her name, using uppercase and lowercase letters, on the paper-covered lid.

Fill the jar with cookies that they have helped to make.

OATMEAL MIX-IT-UP COOKIES

Oatmeal Mix-It-Up Cookies are delicious treats that can be put in the children's cookie jars.

Skills to Teach

Teach children 2 years old and up:

- How to work with dough
- How to read names
- To become familiar with their own last name

Materials List

- A large bowl and a wooden spoon
- 1 cup flour
- 2 cups quick-cooking oatmeal
- 1 cup brown sugar
- 1 cup margarine (2 sticks) at room temperature
- 1 teaspoon baking soda
- A small drinking glass
- A cereal bowl halfway full of sugar

Directions

Put aprons on everyone and gather them around the kitchen table. The children can measure the flour, oatmeal, brown sugar, margarine, and baking soda into the large bowl.

They can mix the dough by squeezing it with their hands until it is blended, or by using the wooden spoon. Then they can pinch off pieces of dough, rolling them into 1-inch balls and placing them on an ungreased cookie sheet.

Next they should press each cookie flat, but not too flat, with the bottom of the small glass dipped in sugar. When all cookies have been flattened, bake in a preheated 350°F oven for 10 minutes.

While the cookies are baking, print the children's first and last names on a paper plate, one for each child. Use uppercase and lowercase letters. Then hold up a plate so the children can see the name. Ask, "Whose plate is this? If this is your name, raise your hand." This is a good game even if you are working with only one child. Seeing his first and last name helps him grow accustomed to how it looks and to the letters that are in it. It also teaches him his last name, if he doesn't already know it.

When the cookies are baked, let each child take his share from the baking sheet with a spatula, putting the cookies on his own paper plate.

BAKING BREAD

Baking bread is a wonderful treat. The bread smells good and is good to eat. Dough is like clay that tastes just great. Turn it into a creative shape!

Skills to Teach

Teach children 2 years old and up:

- To sit still, listen, and follow directions
- How to measure, stir, and bake
- To be creative with dough
- How bread is made

Materials List

- A large bowl and a wooden spoon
- One or two greased baking sheets
- 2¼ cups lukewarm water
- 2 packages active dry yeast
- 7¼ cups flour, divided into 2 piles
- 3 tablespoons sugar
- 1 tablespoon salt
- 2 tablespoons vegetable shortening

Directions

Help the children measure the lukewarm water into the bowl. They can stir in the yeast, one-half of the flour, the sugar, salt, and vegetable shortening. Let them take turns stirring this mixture until it is smooth.

Add and mix in the rest of the flour to make a stiff dough. Put the dough on a tabletop or breadboard with a little extra flour to keep it from sticking. Knead it by folding it over and pressing down hard with the heel of your hand. Keep kneading it for 10 minutes, until it forms a smooth elastic ball. The children will love to help you if you get tired.

Grease a large bowl with shortening. Put the dough in the bowl. Turn the dough upside down to grease its top. Cover the bowl with plastic wrap to keep the dough from drying out, and set it in a warm place for 1¹/₂ hours.

Punch the dough down with your fingers and turn it over. Cover it again and let it rise for 30 minutes.

Put aprons on the children and seat them around the kitchen table. Give each child a small pile of flour that they can spread around in front of them. Tell them not to clap their hands.

Give each child a portion of dough. They can play with it as long as they wish; lots of kneading only makes better bread. When they tire of playing with the dough they can shape it in many ways, such as a round loaf, a long loaf, a baseball and bat, a dough boy, a basket with eggs, a bird's nest with eggs, or whatever.

The children can place their creations on the greased baking sheets. Let the dough rise for 1 hour.

Bake in a preheated oven at 425 °F for 20 minutes, or until the bread is a rich golden brown. As soon as the bread comes out of the oven, brush it with soft shortening or butter for a soft, glowing crust.

September

In this chapter the children are repeatedly exposed to shapes, letters, phonics, and numbers in a concentrated collection of learning crafts. Projects include several shapes pictures, alphabet games to make and bake, and a Paper Plate Self.

More Teach 'n Travel

We can teach colors to children all day. With the number of traffic lights that stop us when we drive, our children should know the colors *red* and *green* by the age of 2. Yellow traffic lights aren't very useful for teaching, however, because they stay on such a short time. Besides, sometimes they are orange.

To teach red and green, however, each time you pull up to a red light, say, "Look! A red light! We have to stop." Children will learn readily this way. When the light turns green, say, "Green light! Now we can go."

Remember that the children in your car cannot escape your teaching. They are the classic "captive audience." You can teach them numbers by pointing out signs along the road. Say, "Look! That sign says *35*." The next time you see one, say, "Liz, there's another sign with a *3* and a *5*. What number is that?" If Liz doesn't know it's a *35*, tell her. Then ask immediately, "What number was that? 35. That's right, Liz."

Craft-Training Skills to Learn

The children will feel like they are going to school with their older friends by the time they finish this chapter. September Craft-training skills include:

- Matching uppercase and lower-case letters of the alphabet
- Learning phonics with a sound box
- Counting and reading numbers
- Learning the meaning of *left*, *right*, *above*, *behind*, and *extends*
- Learning to write his or her first and last name
- Learning to write other words like *School Bus* and *Truck*
- Plenty of practice in drawing, cutting, and gluing
- Learning the names of the colors and shapes

APPLE TREE AND HOUSE PICTURE

This craft has shapes and colors, too. It teaches how to cut and glue (FIG. 9-1).

Skills to Teach

Teach children 2 years old and up:

- The colors *blue*, *brown*, *red*, *green*, and *yellow*
- The *rectangle*, *square*, *circle*, and *triangle* shapes
- To count to 6
- Drawing skills
- Gluing skills
- How to write his or her first and last name

Teach children 4 years old and up:

- Cutting skills
- The meaning of *left*, *right*, and *above*

Materials List

- Construction paper in the following colors: light blue, dark blue, brown, red, green, and yellow
- A ruler and a pencil
- Crayons or narrow-tipped markers
- Scissors
- Glue

9-1 The Apple Tree and House Picture

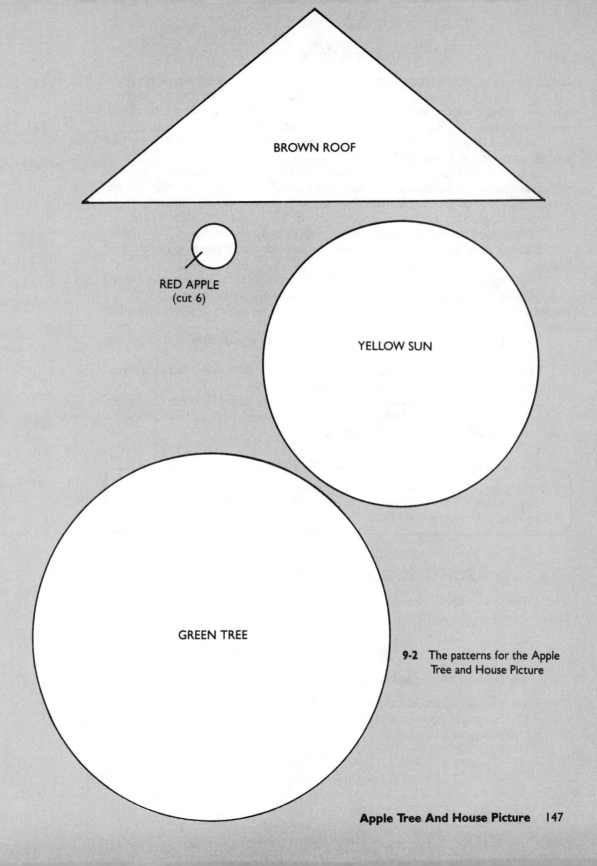

BROWN ROOF

RED APPLE
(cut 6)

YELLOW SUN

GREEN TREE

9-2 The patterns for the Apple
Tree and House Picture

Directions

For each picture, use the pencil and ruler to draw a 1-×-3-inch brown rectangle, a 1-×-1¹/2-inch red rectangle, and a 4-×-4-inch dark square. Use the pattern to trace a brown triangle roof, a green circle tree, a yellow circle sun, and six small red circles for apples (FIG. 9-2). Repeat this step for each child.

Cut these shapes out for younger children. Encourage children 4 years old and up to cut out the shapes after you have drawn them.

Each child should have a set of shapes and a sheet of light blue paper on which to glue them. Instruct the children by saying, "*First*, glue the *blue square* on the *right* side of your paper near the bottom to make a house.

"*Second*, glue the *brown triangle above* the *blue square* to make a roof.

"*Third*, glue the *red rectangle* on the roof to make a chimney.

"*Fourth*, glue the *brown rectangle* on the *left* side of the paper to make a tree trunk.

"*Fifth*, glue the *green circle above* the tree trunk to make the top of the tree.

"Count the *red circle* apples to see how many you have. One . . . two . . . three . . . four . . . five . . . six. How many red circle apples do you have? *Six!* Glue these onto the apple tree.

"Glue the *yellow circle above* the house and tree to make the sun. Now use crayons or markers to finish your picture."

The children might want to draw a person to live in the house. They can draw doors and windows, and smoke coming out of the chimney.

When he is finished drawing, each child should turn his paper over and print his first and last name on the back of the paper. Make sure they hold the pencils or markers correctly when they write and draw.

woolie-pullie

Before giving your child a whole apple, push a popsicle stick through the bottom to make it easier to hold and more fun to eat. Chinese chopsticks make wonderful long handles for Apples-On-A-Stick.

SCHOOL BUS SHAPES PICTURE

The children can draw their older brothers and sisters in this School Bus, and learn while they draw (FIG. 9-3).

Skills to Teach

Teach children 2 years old and up:

- The colors *yellow, black, orange,* and *white*
- The *rectangle, square,* and *circle* shapes
- Drawing skills
- Gluing skills

9-3 The School Bus Shapes Picture

Teach children 4 years old and up:

- Cutting skills
- How to write the word *School Bus*

Materials List

- Yellow, black, and orange construction paper
- White (typing) paper
- A ruler and pencil
- Crayons or narrow-tipped markers
- Scissors
- Glue

Directions

For each picture, use a pencil and ruler to draw a yellow rectangle 8 × 12 inches, a yellow square 4 × 4 inches, and three white rectangles 2 × 3 inches. Use the pattern in FIG. 9-4 to trace two large black circles and two smaller orange circles.

Cut these shapes out. Encourage children 4 years old and up to cut their own shapes after you have drawn them.

Give each child a set of shapes. Instruct the children by saying, "To make a bus, glue the *yellow square* onto the end of the *yellow rectangle*."

"Glue the *2 large black circles* on the bus to make tires. Glue the *small orange circles* on top of the black tires to make hubcaps."

"Draw a boy or girl on the *3 white rectangles*. Glue them on the bus to make windows with children looking out."

"Now use your crayons or markers to draw a driver for the bus. Print the words *School Bus* on the side of the bus.

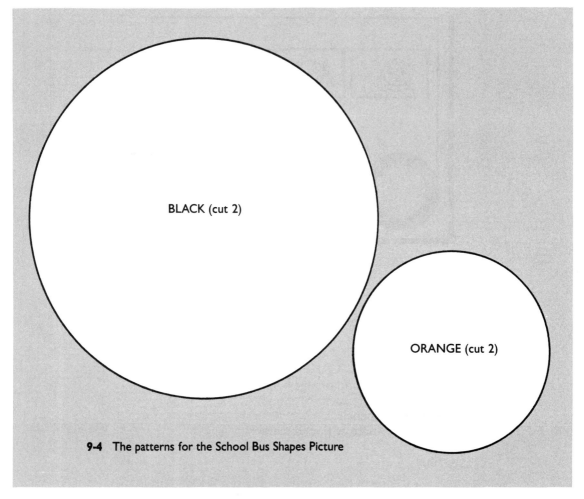

BLACK (cut 2)

ORANGE (cut 2)

9-4 The patterns for the School Bus Shapes Picture

TRUCK SHAPES PICTURE

Children are fascinated by trucks of all kinds. They'll enjoy making a picture of trucks, and they'll learn shapes, too (FIG. 9-5).

Skills to Teach

Teach children 2 years old and up:

- The colors *red*, *black*, *brown*, and *blue*
- The *rectangle*, *square*, *circle*, and *triangle* shapes
- Drawing skills
- Gluing skills

9-5 The Truck Shapes Picture

Teach children 4 years old and up:

- Cutting skills
- How to write the word *truck*
- The meaning of many words such as *left*, *right*, *narrow*, *extends*, and *behind*

Materials List

- Red, black, brown, and blue construction paper
- A ruler and pencil
- Scissors
- Glue
- Crayons or narrow-tipped markers

Directions

For each picture, use the pencil and ruler to draw a brown rectangle 3 × 8 inches, a skinny brown rectangle 1/4 × 8 inches, a red rectangle 4 × 6 inches, and a red square 2 × 2 inches. Use the pattern to trace a black triangle roof and two black circle wheels (FIG. 9-6).

Cut these shapes out for younger children. Encourage children 4 years old and up to do their own cutting after you draw the shapes for them.

Give each child a set of shapes and a sheet of blue construction paper on which to assemble the picture. Instruct the children by saying: "*First*, glue the *large brown rectangle* on the *right* side of the *blue* paper to make a tall building.

"*Second*, glue the *red rectangle* next to the tall building. Glue the *red square* on the *left* side of the red rectangle to make a truck.

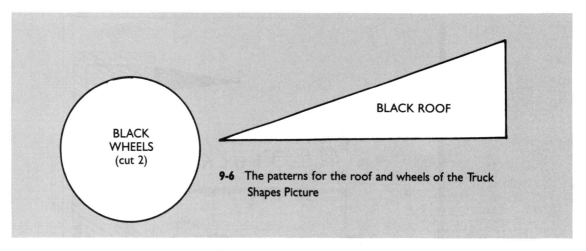

9-6 The patterns for the roof and wheels of the Truck Shapes Picture

"*Third*, glue *two black circle* tires to the bottom of the truck. Glue the skinny *brown rectangle* below the tires to make a road.

"*Fourth*, print the word *Truck* on the side of the truck.

"*Fifth*, glue the *black triangle* roof on the side of the building so that it *extends over* the truck. Now use crayons or markers to finish your picture. You might draw a person driving the truck with engine exhaust coming from *behind* it. You can add windows to the building, too."

PAPER SAUCER FACE

Shown in FIG. 9-7, the Paper Saucer Face is a delightful project to do with your children.

Skills to Teach

Teach children 2 years old and up:

- The colors *brown*, *black*, *blue*, *red*, and *pink*
- Gluing skills
- The *circle* and *rectangle* shapes

Teach children 5 years old and up:

- Cutting skills
- The meaning of many words such as *larger* and *smaller*, *first*, *second*, and *third*

Materials List

- 6-inch paper saucers, plain white
- Brown, black, blue, red, and pink construction paper
- A pencil and ruler
- Scissors
- Glue

9-7 The Paper Saucer Face

Directions

For each face, use the pencil and ruler to draw two brown rectangles $1^1/2 \times 6$ inches and a brown rectangle 2×4 inches. Trace the pattern in FIG. 9-8 to make two blue circle eyes, two black circle eyeballs, two pink cheeks, a pink circle nose, and a red mouth.

Cut the shapes out for younger children. Encourage children 5 years old and up to cut their own after you have drawn them.

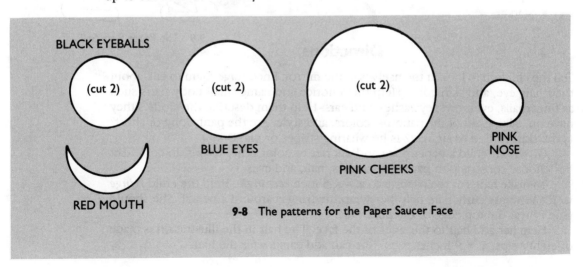

BLACK EYEBALLS

(cut 2)

(cut 2)

(cut 2)

PINK NOSE

BLUE EYES

PINK CHEEKS

RED MOUTH

9-8 The patterns for the Paper Saucer Face

Give each child the cutout pieces, a paper saucer, and glue. Then tell them the following: *"First, fringe* the two *larger brown rectangles* the long way to make hair. Curl the hair by wrapping the fringes tightly around a pencil.

"*Second*, fringe the *smaller brown rectangle* the short way, curling it around a pencil to form bangs. Glue the brown hair and bangs onto the paper saucer.

"*Third*, glue on the *blue circle* eyes. Glue the *black circle* eyeballs on the blue eyes.

"*Fourth*, glue the *red* mouth on the Paper Saucer Face. Add the *two pink circle* cheeks and the *pink circle* nose.

"*Fifth*, use crayons to draw on eyelashes and eyebrows."

PAPER PLATE SELF

This person can have your hands, feet, and nose. Give her your eyes and even your clothes! (FIG. 9-9)

Skills to Teach

Teach children 3 years old and up:

- Body awareness (What do I look like?)
- The *circle*, *rectangle*, and *oval* shapes
- Construction skills and how to use their imagination
- Tracing, cutting, and gluing

Materials List

- A mirror so the child can see herself
- 9-inch white paper plate
- 9-×-12-inch construction paper in various colors
- Scissors
- Glue
- Markers

9-9 The Paper Plate Self

Directions

Tell the children to look at themselves in the mirror. Encourage them to talk about their hair, eye, and skin color. Help them notice and name small body parts such as fingernails, eyebrows, eyelashes, and ears. Help them describe the clothes they have on, talking about the patterns, colors, and style. Are the pants long or short? Is the skirt ruffled or straight? Is he wearing stripes or plaid?

Give each child a paper plate and ask her to color it her own skin color. Let her choose construction paper for clothes, hair, and eyes.

To make hair, cut the paper into a 3-×-5-inch *rectangle*. Help the child *fringe* it. If she wants curly hair, help her wrap the fringes around a pencil. She should glue it near the top edge of the plate face.

Help her add hair to the sides of the face. The hair in the illustration is made of eight strips, 1 × 9 inches each. She can add ears *under* the hair.

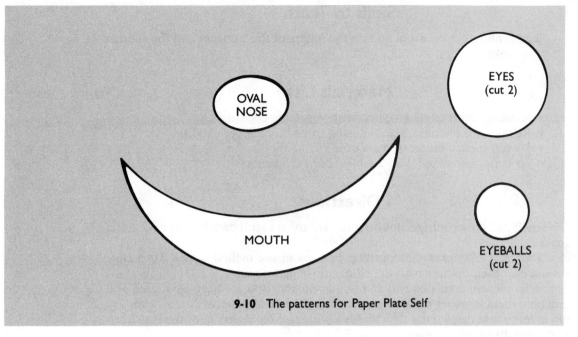

9-10 The patterns for Paper Plate Self

For the younger child, trace and cut out eyes, eyeballs, nose, and mouth from the patterns provided (FIG. 9-10). Encourage children 4 years old and up to trace and cut their own. Tell the child to glue on eyes of her own eye color, black eyeballs, an *oval* nose, and a mouth.

Help the child glue a 9-×-12-inch sheet of construction paper on the bottom of the plate face to make a body.

To make arms and legs, fold a 9-×-12-inch sheet of paper in half lengthwise. Fold it in half again lengthwise and cut on the creases to make four 2¼-×-12-inch rectangles.

Tell the child to glue two *rectangles* on the body to make arms, and two *rectangles* on the bottom of the body to make legs.

To make hands, fold a piece of paper in half. Trace around the child's hand. Cut out both thicknesses of paper together. Let children who are 5 years old cut this themselves. The child can glue the hands on the ends of the arms. Repeat this to make feet by tracing around the child's foot or shoe. Glue feet on the ends of the legs.

Now, she can use scraps of paper and markers to add all kinds of things to her Paper Plate Self. These might include buttons, barrettes, belt, jewelry, and so forth. If you have scraps of cloth, real buttons, fake flowers, or ribbons, let her glue and tape them to decorate her Self.

BISCUIT ALPHABET

Just as you used biscuits to teach shapes, you can also use them to teach the alphabet and the sounds the letters make.

Skills to Teach

Teach children 2 years old and up the letters of the alphabet and the sounds they make.

Materials List

- A baking sheet or two, coated with vegetable cooking spray
- Refrigerator biscuits. (Plan on using three biscuits per child.)
- 1/4 cup melted butter or margarine
- 1/2 cup sugar mixed with 2 tablespoons cinnamon

Directions

Give each child three refrigerator biscuits. Tell them to roll each biscuit into a long snake.

They can take turns dipping their biscuits in the melted butter. Then they should coat their biscuits with the cinnamon-sugar mixture.

Help the children place their biscuits on the baking sheet, arranging and pinching them together to form letters. They could make a letter that you are trying to teach that day, a letter the child is having trouble learning, or the first letter in the child's name.

To teach phonics with Biscuit Alphabets, comment, "I like the *M* you're making, Mary. How does the *M* sound? It sounds like this, doesn't it? M−m−m−m. Can you think of some words that start with the *M* sound?" Help her think of a few *M* words. Emphasize the beginning *M* sound by repeating the words you both think of. For instance, M−m−m−mary, m−m−m−mommy, m−m−m−mouse.

Bake in a preheated oven at 400 °F for 10 minutes. Take the letters off the baking sheet immediately and let them cool on a cooling rack or a piece of foil.

ALPHABET CLOTHESLINE

The Alphabet Clothesline is a great tool to teach children about uppercase and lowercase letters (FIG. 9-11).

Skills to Teach

Teach children 2 years old and up to match the uppercase and lowercase letters of the alphabet.

Materials List

- Two chairs
- A piece of string or rope 8′ long. (You can use anything from clothesline to kite string.)
- Typing paper
- Construction paper

- Scissors
- Markers or crayons
- A stapler
- 26 clip clothespins

Directions

Tie the rope or string between two chairs, making it taut. Cut 26 rectangles $3\frac{1}{2}$ × 4 inches from typing paper. Use a marker or crayons to print the uppercase letters of the alphabet, one on each rectangle.

Fold down $\frac{1}{2}$ inch at the top of each rectangle. Place this fold over the Clothesline and staple the rectangle in place. Do this with all 26 letters, stapling them up in alphabetical order so they look like clothes hanging on a line.

Now cut 26 rectangular strips $1\frac{1}{2}$ × 6 inches from construction paper. Fold each in half crosswise. Print the lowercase letters of the alphabet, one on each strip.

To play this game, each child picks any lowercase letter and hunts along the Clothesline until he finds the matching uppercase letter. If they say the alphabet out loud as they hunt, they will find the letters faster. They will also learn alphabetical order as they play.

Then they clip the lowercase letter over its partner with a clothespin. A child can play this game alone, but the spirit of competition makes playing it with a friend or two more fun. He can also play with an adult who has suddenly developed amnesia.

9-11 The Alphabet Clothesline

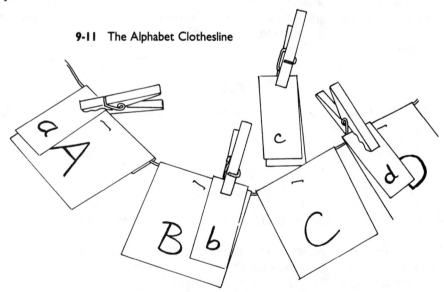

A SOUND BOX

A Sound Box can be made for any letter or combination of letters in the alphabet. Its purpose is to teach children the sound a letter makes (phonics) in a fun and interesting way (FIG. 9-12).

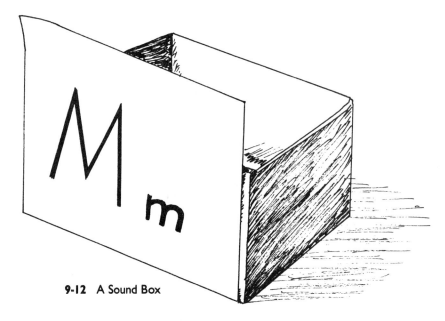

9-12 A Sound Box

Skills to Teach

Teach children 2 years old and up beginning phonics, or how a letter sounds at the beginning of a word.

Teach children 6 years old and up advanced phonics—how a letter sounds at the end of a word, or consonant blends such as *th*, *ch*, and *sh* at the beginning or end of a word.

Materials List

- An empty cardboard box, such as a large shoebox
- Construction paper
- Markers
- Glue

Directions

Select a letter that you want to teach the children. The letter *M* is a good one to do first.

Use the markers to print both the uppercase and lowercase form of the letter on construction paper. Glue the paper to the front of the cardboard box.

Tell the children, "This is the letter *M*. What letter is it?"

The children say, "*M*."

Then say, "The letter *M* sounds like this, m−m−m−m. Can you think of anything that starts with the *M* sound?"

If the children can't, give them some examples, "How about m−m−m−marker?" Put the marker in the Sound Box. "Let's all say m−m−m−marker."

The children respond, "M−m−m−marker."

Then say, "Let's look around the playroom and find more things that start with the *M* sound." Walk slowly around the room, saying m−m−m as if to yourself, but loud enough for everyone to hear you. Soon the children will be making the *M* sound, too.

Help them find about 10 items that start with *M*, and put them in the Sound Box. Then pull out each item and say its name, heavily emphasizing the *M* sound.

See if the children can take turns saying the names of the items just as you did.

Leave the Box in a place where the children can play with the *M* toys.

After about three days, take off the construction paper *M* page, and repeat this game with a new sound, such as *S*.

CYLINDER SOLDIER

Any cylinder can be used to make this wonderful soldier (FIG. 9-13). These measurements are for a Pringles potato chip can soldier.

Skills to Teach

Teach children 4 years old and up:

- The letters *X* and *L*
- The colors *yellow, red, blue, white,* and *black*
- The *rectangle* and *square* shapes
- Measuring 1/2 cup
- Following directions

Teach children 8 years old and up:

- How to measure with a ruler
- Precise cutting skills
- The word *epaulet*

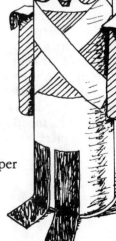

Materials List

- 1/2 cup beans to make the can heavier
- A Pringles potato chip can
- Yellow, red, blue, white, and black construction paper
- Ruler
- Pencil
- Scissors
- Glue
- Paper punch

Directions

9-13 Cylinder Soldier

Measure 1/2 cup beans into the empty can. Put on the lid. Help children 8 years old and older to measure and cut all the rectangles and squares needed for this craft. This takes awhile, and they may want to prepare these shapes the day before making the soldier. Younger children should have the next step done for them.

Use the ruler, pencil, and scissors to measure, draw, and cut out the following:

(1) $2^1/2$-×-10-inch yellow rectangle for the face
(1) 3-×-10-inch red rectangle for the shirt
(1) $4^1/2$-×-10-inch blue rectangle for the pants
(2) 1-×-$5^1/2$-inch white rectangles for the letter X
(1) 5-×-12-inch black rectangle for the hat
(1) $1/2$-×-12-inch red rectangle for the hat band
(2) 4-inch red squares for the arms
(2) 2-inch red squares for the epaulets
(2) 1-×-3-inch black rectangles for the boots

Tell the children to make sure all the paper seams are in one place to create a smooth front side for their soldier. Then instruct the children by saying:

"Glue the yellow rectangle at the top of the can, just below the lid. This is the face.

"Glue the large red rectangle below the face and overlapping it slightly. This is the shirt.

"Glue the blue rectangle at the bottom of the can, slightly overlapping the red. These are the pants.

"Glue the two white rectangles to form the letter X. Glue the X in the middle of the shirt. It will extend onto the face a little and down onto the pants.

"Squirt a line of glue $1/2$ inch below the lid. Wrap the large black rectangle around the top of the can to make a hat. Press the bottom edge of the hat into the glue to make it hold firmly. Glue the back seam closed but leave the hat open at the top.

"Glue the narrow red rectangle around the base of the hat for a hat band.

"Roll the two red squares into cylinders. Overlap slightly and glue closed. These are arms. Apply glue to the outside of each arm seam. Press one arm on each side of the shirt, just below the face.

"Cut fringes $3/4$ inches long on one side of each yellow square. Bend the fringes down to make epaulets. Use your finger to put glue on the thin edge of each arm cylinder. Lay an *epaulet* (ornamental fringed shoulder pad) on top of each arm with the fringes hanging down the sides. They will stick to the glue and will dry in place.

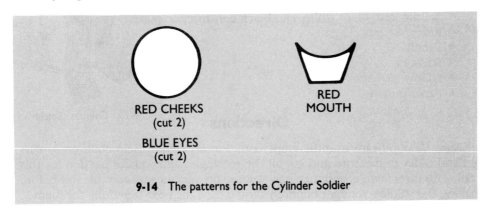

RED CHEEKS
(cut 2)

BLUE EYES
(cut 2)

RED
MOUTH

9-14 The patterns for the Cylinder Soldier

"Bend the small black rectangles 3/4 inch into the letter *L*. Apply glue to the back of each *L*. Glue them close together on the front of the pants to make boots. The bottom of the *L* is the foot of the boot.

"If you wish, use the pattern (FIG. 9-14) to add red circle cheeks, blue circle eyes, and a red mouth to your soldier. Use the paper punch to make two black eyeballs."

MAGIC WATER PICTURES

Change your drawings to a sparkling wonder. Just brush with Magic Water!

Skills to Teach

Teach children 4 years old and up:

- Coloring skills
- What *crystals* look like

Materials List

- 1 cup Epsom salt (Buy this in a drugstore.)
- 1 cup water
- A small pot for the stove
- Construction paper in dark colors of black, purple, or blue
- Crayons
- A wide watercolor brush

Directions

Before working with the children, combine 1 cup Epsom salt (magnesium sulfate) and 1 cup water in a pot. Heat to boiling, and stir until the Epsom salt has dissolved. Let this cool.

The children can draw pictures or designs using light crayons and dark construction paper. Then they can brush the cool Magic Water over their entire picture. Set these aside to dry.

As the Epsom salt solution dries, it forms beautiful feathery crystals on the paper. The crystals show up best on dark paper.

Magic Water can also be colored with a few drops of food color. Brush it over pictures drawn on white paper for a sparkly look.

GRANDMA'S PEANUT BUTTER COOKIES

Peanut Butter Cookies are a favorite of children. You can use them to teach, as well as to treat.

Skills to Teach

Teach children 2 years old and up:

- To sit still, listen, and follow directions
- How to measure, stir, and bake
- How to work with dough
- How to read his or her name

Materials List

- 1 cup margarine or butter
- 1$\frac{1}{4}$ cups brown sugar
- 1$\frac{1}{4}$ cups white sugar
- Two eggs
- 1 cup peanut butter
- 1$\frac{1}{4}$ teaspoons vanilla extract
- 2$\frac{1}{2}$ cups flour
- 2 teaspoons baking powder
- 1$\frac{1}{4}$ teaspoons baking soda
- $\frac{1}{4}$ teaspoon salt
- A large bowl and a wooden spoon
- A cookie sheet
- A fork and a little bowl of flour
- Paper plates and a marker

Directions

Help the children measure the butter, the brown sugar, and the white granulated sugar into a large bowl. They should take turns stirring with a wooden spoon until they are blended.

The children can crack the two eggs into a saucer, then add them to the dough. Stir again until blended.

Help them measure the peanut butter and vanilla, adding it to the bowl. Stir well.

Help the children measure the flour, baking powder, baking soda, and salt, and add it to the dough. They can take turns stirring again until the dough is smooth. Refrigerate the dough for 30 minutes.

While the dough is chilling, play the Read-Your-Name Game. (See "November" crafts.)

After the dough is chilled, put a portion on each child's plate. They can pinch off pieces the size of a walnut, roll them into balls, and place them on an ungreased cookie sheet.

Show the children how to flatten each cookie slightly with a fork dipped in a little bowl of flour so it won't stick to the dough. The should press each cookie twice, making a crisscross design.

Bake in a preheated oven at 400 °F for about 10 minutes, or until light brown around the edges.

Give each child the spatula and let him transfer his own cookies to his plate to eat or share.

October

Halloween crafts occupy the entire month while the children practice following directions, eye-hand coordination, counting skills, and recognition of shapes and colors. Three spooky recipes for making Spider Bread, Witches Fingers, and Witches Bones are included.

Children Are Creative

Children love to make things, and they don't have the reservations about experimenting that we adults do. If the product turns out a little odd looking, their attitude is, "So what?". The process of making it was fun, and they're willing to try again. Next time the product will probably turn out better.

Once you work on crafts with your children, they will want to create by themselves. Establish rules so the mess will be less for you. Make sure they paint or glue only in the kitchen with newspapers under their work. They would rather make crafts in the middle of their bed or on your coffee table, so you must be strict. Make sure they clean up their own messes unless you have a live-in maid.

Then make craft materials available to them. Scissors, school glue, paper, crayons, and markers can be kept in a box under your watchful eye. You can loan it out when asked. Your children may become so enthusiastic about creating things that they will give up television for a change.

Craft-Training Skills to Learn

October crafts introduce the children to the idea of alphabetical order as they follow step A, step B, step C, etc. They learn how to use paper fasteners, and how to fringe and pleat.

Other Craft-training skills to practice include:

- Learning to recognize colors and shapes
- Learning the meaning of *large*, *medium*, *small*, *tall*, *short*, *next to*, and *unfold*
- Putting things together

- Writing his or her name
- Drawing a face
- Counting to 10
- Gluing, drawing, and cutting skills

BLACK CAT

This cat has diamonds and rectangles, too. I'll learn my shapes before you say, "BOO!" (FIG. 10-1).

Skills to Teach

Teach children 2 years old and up:

- The *triangle, rectangle,* and *diamond* shapes
- The colors *black, green,* and *orange*
- Gluing skills

Teach children 4 years old and up:

- Cutting skills
- Assembling skills: putting things together

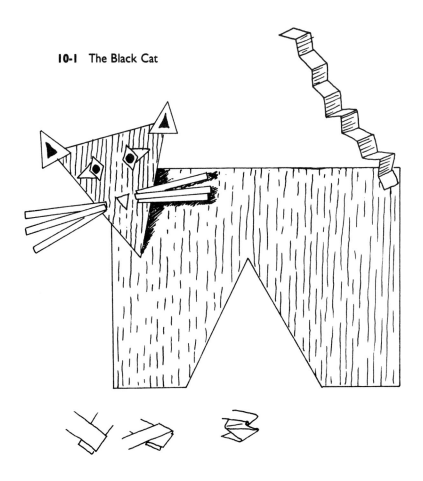

10-1 The Black Cat

Materials List

- Black, green, and orange construction paper
- A ruler and pencil
- Scissors
- Glue
- A black marker

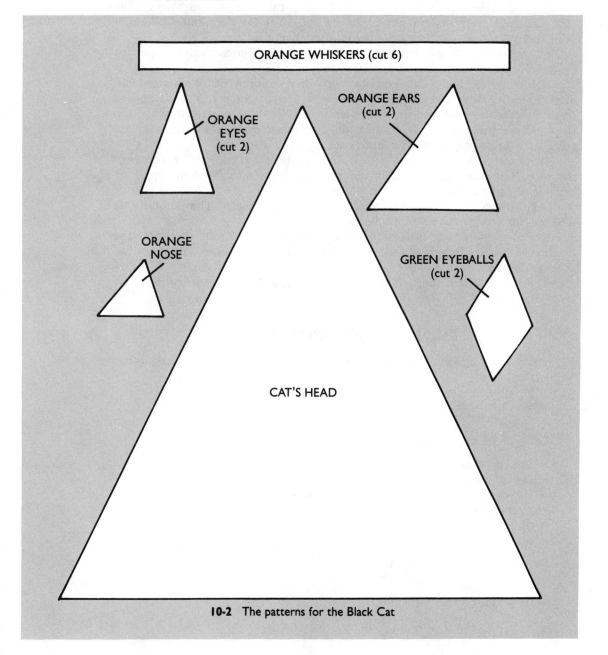

ORANGE WHISKERS (cut 6)

ORANGE EYES (cut 2)

ORANGE EARS (cut 2)

ORANGE NOSE

GREEN EYEBALLS (cut 2)

CAT'S HEAD

10-2 The patterns for the Black Cat

Directions

For each cat, cut a 1-×-4-inch strip from the short side of a sheet of black construction paper. Cut this strip in half, forming two 1-×-4^1/$_2$-inch strips for the cat's neck.

Use the pattern in FIG. 10-2 to draw a triangle cat's head on the bottom of each black rectangle that is left. Cut out the triangle, leaving the cat's legs and body.

Use the pattern to draw six orange whiskers, two orange eyes, two orange ears, an orange nose, and two green eyeballs (FIG. 10-2). Cut them out. Children 4 years old and up can cut their own if you draw them first.

Cut a 1-×-9-inch strip from another sheet of black construction paper for each cat's tail.

Making the neck is a little complex for young children, but it's a nice technique to learn. To make the neck, lay the two strips at right angles to each other, one on top of the other to form the letter *L*. Fold the bottom strip over the top strip and press down. Repeat, folding the strips upon each other until they are completely folded together. Glue both ends together.

When the neck is finished, tell each child to glue it to the *upper-left corner* of the body. Help them glue the *black triangle* head to the neck, with the tip of the triangle pointing down, as shown in FIG. 10-1.

Tell them to fold the *black rectangle* tail into 1-inch pleats. They should glue it to the *upper-right corner* of the body.

Next they should add the *orange triangle* ears. They can color them with the black marker. They should add the *orange triangle* eyes and nose. Then they can glue on the *green diamond* eyeballs.

Their Black Cat is finished when they have glued on six *orange rectangle* whiskers.

DANCING PUMPKIN MAN

I can make the pumpkin dance, one, two, three, as I learn my shapes as easy as can be! (FIG. 10-3).

Skills to Teach

Teach children 2 years old and up:

- The colors *orange*, *black*, and *green*
- The *triangle*, *circle*, and *rectangle* shapes
- The meaning of *large*, *medium*, and *small*
- To count to *4*
- Gluing skills
- Drawing skills

Teach children 4 years old and up:

- Cutting skills
- How to use paper fasteners

Materials List

- Orange, black, and green construction paper
- A black water-based marker, narrow-tipped
- Scissors
- Glue
- Five spread-apart paper fasteners

Directions

For each Dancing Pumpkin Man, use the patterns in FIGS. 10-4 and 10-5 to draw one orange body, one orange head, two orange jack-o'-lanterns, four $1^{1}/_{2}$-×-3-inch orange rectangles for arms and legs, one $^{1}/_{2}$-×-1-inch green rectangle for a stem, and two black feet.

Cut them out for younger children. Encourage children 4 years old and up to cut their own shapes after you have traced them.

Give the shapes and a black marker to the children. Instruct them by saying "*First*, draw lines on the *large orange circle* to make it look like a pumpkin.

"*Second*, draw a jack-o'-lantern face on the *medium-sized orange circle* to make a head for the Dancing Pumpkin Man.

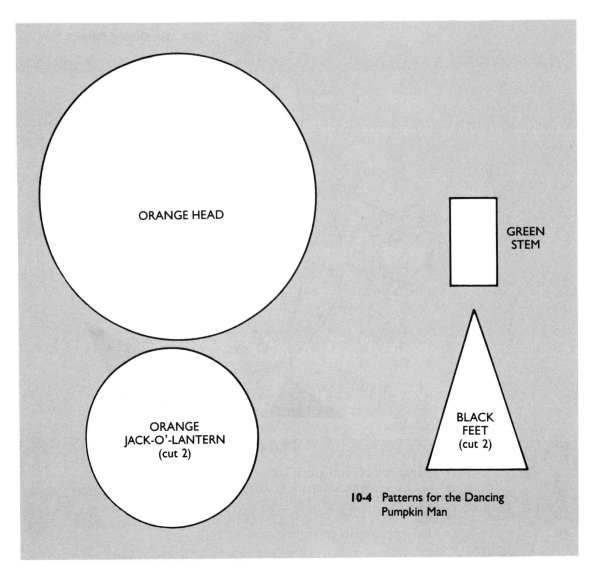

ORANGE HEAD

GREEN STEM

ORANGE JACK-O'-LANTERN (cut 2)

BLACK FEET (cut 2)

10-4 Patterns for the Dancing Pumpkin Man

"*Third,* draw jack-o'-lantern faces on the *two small orange circles.*

"*Fourth,* use the spread-apart paper fasteners to attach the Pumpkin Man's head to his body." Many children will need help with these fasteners.

"How many *orange rectangles* do you have? Let's count them together and see." Count out loud with the children. "One . . . two . . . three . . . four. How many orange rectangles do you have? *Four.*" Help the children fasten the four orange rectangles to the Pumpkin Man's body to make arms and legs. Use the paper fasteners as shown in FIG. 10-3.

"Glue the *small green rectangle* to the top of the Pumpkin Man's head for a stem. Glue the *two small orange* jack-o'-lanterns on the ends of the arms. Glue the *two black triangles* on the ends of the legs to make feet.

"Make your Pumpkin Man dance by moving his arms and legs."

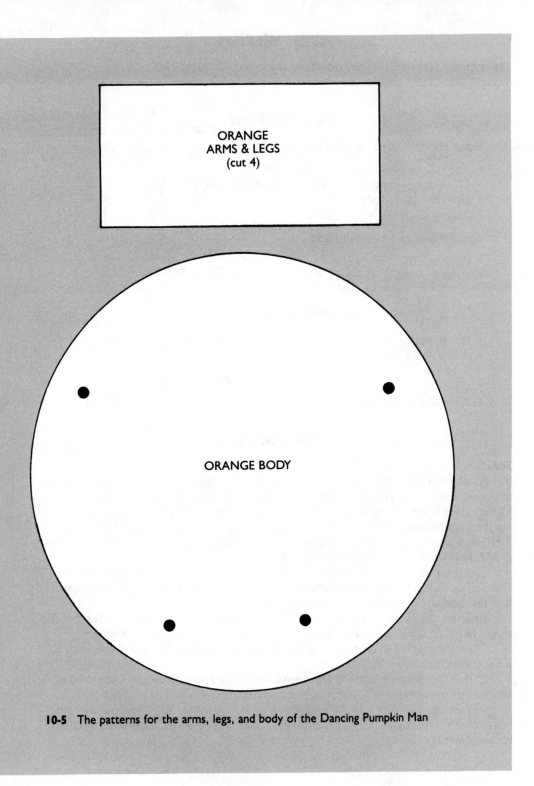

10-5 The patterns for the arms, legs, and body of the Dancing Pumpkin Man

PAPER WITCH

This witch has a wart on the end of her nose, a circle head and triangle toes! (FIG. 10-6).

Skills to Teach

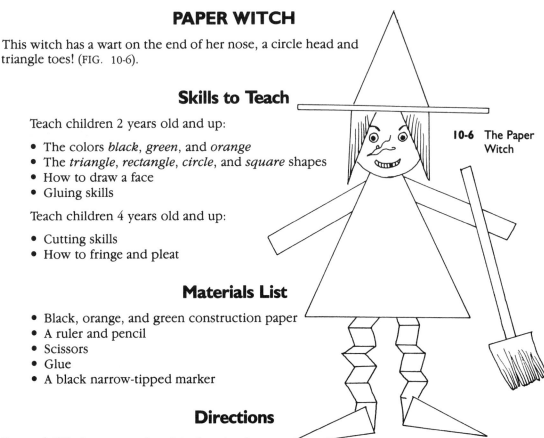

10-6   The Paper Witch

Teach children 2 years old and up:

- The colors *black*, *green*, and *orange*
- The *triangle*, *rectangle*, *circle*, and *square* shapes
- How to draw a face
- Gluing skills

Teach children 4 years old and up:

- Cutting skills
- How to fringe and pleat

Materials List

- Black, orange, and green construction paper
- A ruler and pencil
- Scissors
- Glue
- A black narrow-tipped marker

Directions

For each Witch, cut two 1-×-9-inch strips from a sheet of black construction paper for the Witch's legs. Cut a 9-×-11-×-11-inch triangle from the remaining paper for the body. Use the black scraps that are left to trace two black triangles for hair, two black triangle shoes, two black 1-×-5$\frac{1}{2}$-inch rectangle arms, and a narrow black $\frac{1}{4}$-×-8-inch hat brim (FIG. 10-7).

Trace a green circle face, an orange $\frac{1}{2}$-×-10-inch broomstick and an orange 2-×-2-inch square for the broom's bristles.

Cut these shapes out for children younger than 4 years. Children 4 years old and up can cut their own. Show them how to fringe the two triangles for the hair and the orange square for the broom bristles.

Instruct the children by saying: "Glue the *black triangle* hair and the *black triangle* hat to the *green circle* Witch's face. Add the narrow black hat brim.

"Use the marker to draw a mean witch face, or draw a nice face if you wish to make a nice witch.

"Glue the Witch's head to the top of the *large black triangle*. Glue the two *short black rectangles* to the top of her body for arms.

"*Pleat* the two *long black rectangles* at 1-inch intervals. Glue them to the bottom of the triangle body to form legs." You will need to help them with the measurements.

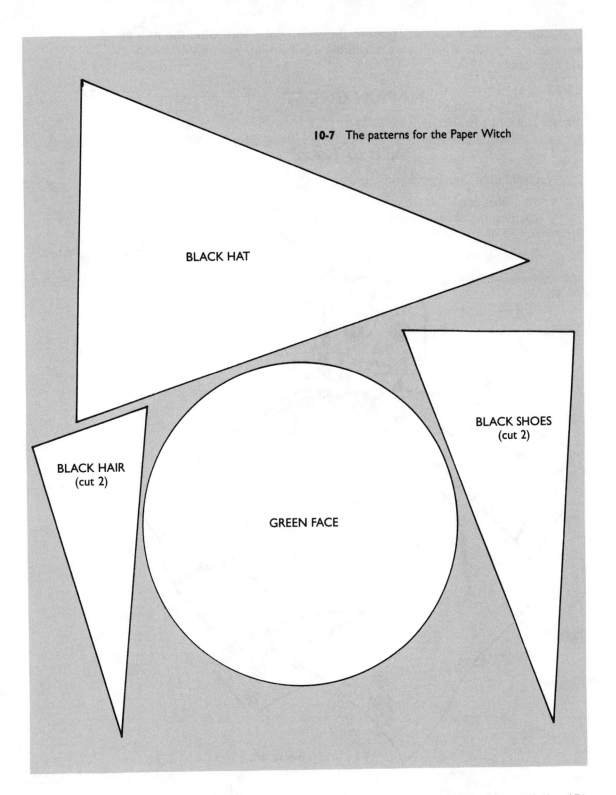

10-7 The patterns for the Paper Witch

BLACK HAT

BLACK SHOES
(cut 2)

BLACK HAIR
(cut 2)

GREEN FACE

"Glue two *black triangle* shoes to the ends of the legs. Glue the *orange* broomstick onto the Witch's arm. Add the *fringed orange square* to the end of the broomstick."

NAPKIN GHOST

I'm not afraid of a napkin ghost! (FIG. 10-8).

Skills to Teach

Teach children 2 years old and up:

- The colors *black* and *white*
- The meaning of *unfold* and *in the center*
- How to draw a face

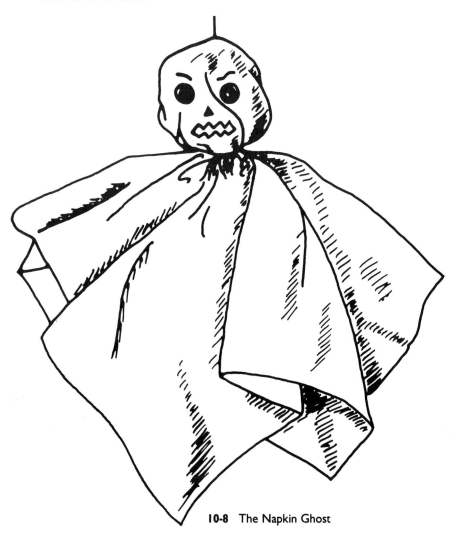

10-8 The Napkin Ghost

Teach children 4 years old and up:

- To follow directions
- How to tie a knot

Materials List

- A white napkin for each ghost (generic napkins work well)
- Two cotton balls for each head
- White thread
- A black skinny marker

Directions

Give each child a napkin, two cotton balls, and a white thread about 24 inches long. Tell them to *unfold* the napkin and lay it flat on the table.

Tell them to put the two *white* cotton balls *in the center* of the *white* napkin. Show them how to pull the napkin up and pinch it shut around the cotton balls to make the ghost's head.

Help them tie the end of the *white* thread around the ghost's neck, just under the cotton balls.

Each child can draw a face on the ghost with the skinny *black* marker.

Hold the ghosts up by the string to make them float around, or tape them in a window or a doorway.

EGG CARTON SPIDER

Egg Carton Spider on a black thread. I'll count his legs and draw on his head! (FIG. 10-9).

Skills to Teach

Teach children 2 years old and up:

- How to draw a face
- To count to *4*
- That spiders have *eight* legs
- To count to *8*

Materials List

- Two 9-inch chenille pipe cleaners or four regular pipe cleaners from the supermarket for each spider
- Scissors
- A Styrofoam egg carton
- A black permanent marker. (A laundry marker.)
- A needle
- Black thread
- Buttons

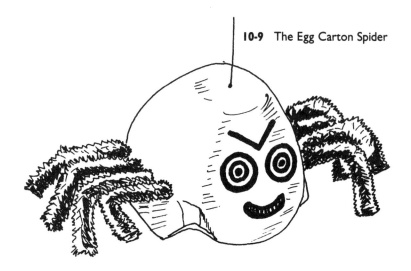

10-9 The Egg Carton Spider

Directions

Cut the chenille pipe cleaners in half with scissors to make four pipe cleaners or cut four regular pipe cleaners into $4^{1/2}$-inch lengths for each spider.

Carefully cut out one eggcup from the Styrofoam egg carton. Children 5 years old and up can cut their own.

Each child can draw a fierce-looking face on the eggcup with the laundry marker.

Give them each four pipe cleaners. Count them out loud with them to make sure that they have the right number.

Talk about spiders. Tell them that spiders have eight legs, while insects have only six legs. Since a spider has eight legs, it is not an insect (bug), but an *arachnid* (uh-RACK-nid). Spiders are in the same class as ticks, scorpions, and mites, all of which have eight legs. You may think this is too much information for a 2-year-old, but it isn't. If he is exposed to such ideas now, he will learn as much as he is ready to learn. This complex idea will not be strange to him when he is introduced to it again at a later age.

Tell your children to turn their eggcup over. Help them insert a pipe cleaner through one side, across the middle of the eggcup, and through the other side so that it extends evenly on both sides of the cup. One pipe cleaner makes two legs. Repeat this step for the remaining three pipe cleaners.

Bend the pipe cleaners downward to look like spider legs. Count the spider legs out loud with each child: "One . . . two . . . three . . . four . . . five . . . six . . . seven . . . eight." Then ask, "How many legs does your spider have? That's right. It has *eight* legs!"

Thread the needle with black thread. Thread the button onto the end of the thread and tie it into place.

Sew the needle through the inside top of each eggcup. Pull it until the button is snug against the inside top. Cut off the needle. The spider now has a black "web" from which to hang.

HALLOWEEN HOUSE PICTURE

I'll learn rectangle, triangle, square, and circle; black, blue, green, orange, and purple! (FIG. 10-10).

Skills to Teach

Teach children 2 years old and up:

- The colors *black*, *blue*, *purple*, *yellow*, *orange*, *green* and *white*
- The names of the *triangle*, *rectangle*, *square*, and *circle* shapes
- Gluing skills
- The meaning of *next to*, *tall*, *short*, *large* and *small*
- How many make *3*
- To count to *4*

Teach children 4 years old and up:

- Cutting skills
- Assembling skills: putting things together
- Alphabetical order

Materials List

- Black, blue, purple, yellow, orange, and green construction paper
- A pencil and ruler
- Scissors
- Glue
- White facial tissue
- A black, narrow-tipped marker

Directions

Each child will use a sheet of black construction paper for the background of this picture. With the pencil and ruler, draw the following for each child:

- ~ Two 1^1/$_2$-×-3^1/$_2$-inch blue rectangles
- ~ One 1^1/$_2$-×-2-inch blue rectangle
- ~ One 3-×-3-inch blue square
- ~ Four ^{1}/$_2$-×-1-inch black rectangles
- ~ Four ^{1}/$_2$-×-^{1}/$_2$-inch black squares
- ~ Two 3-×-3-inch white facial tissue squares
- ~ One ^{1}/$_4$-×-^{1}/$_2$-inch green rectangle

Now use the pattern in FIG. 10-11 to trace a yellow circle moon, an orange circle jack-o'-lantern, three large purple triangle roofs, and one small purple triangle roof for each picture.

10-10 The Halloween House Picture

Cut these shapes out for the children, or let them cut their own if they are at least 4 years old.

Give these pieces to each child. To make the Halloween House Picture, instruct them by saying:

"*A*. Glue the *blue square* near the bottom of the *black* construction paper.

"*B*. Glue the two *tall blue rectangles* next to the *blue square*, one on each side.

"*C*. Glue the *short blue rectangle above* the *blue square*.

"*D*. Glue the *three large purple triangles* above the three *blue rectangles* to make roofs.

"*E*. How many *black rectangles* do you have? Count them with me. One . . . two . . . three . . . four. How many *black* rectangles? *Four*. Glue the *four black rectangles* on the house to make a door and windows.

"*F*. Glue the *small purple triangle* above the *black rectangle* door.

"*G*. How many *black squares* do you have? Let's count them." Count to four out loud with the child. "How many *black squares*? *Four*. Glue these four black squares on both sides of the door to make more windows.

"*H*. Use the black marker to draw a jack-o'-lantern face on the orange circle. Glue the jack-o'-lantern *next to* the house.

"*I*. Add the *small green rectangle* for a pumpkin stem.

"*J*. Glue the *large yellow circle* in the sky for a moon.

"*K*. Pinch each *white* facial tissue square in the middle and squeeze it to make a ghost. Glue the two *white* ghosts near the jack-o'-lantern.

"*L*. Use the black marker to draw tiny faces on the ghosts."

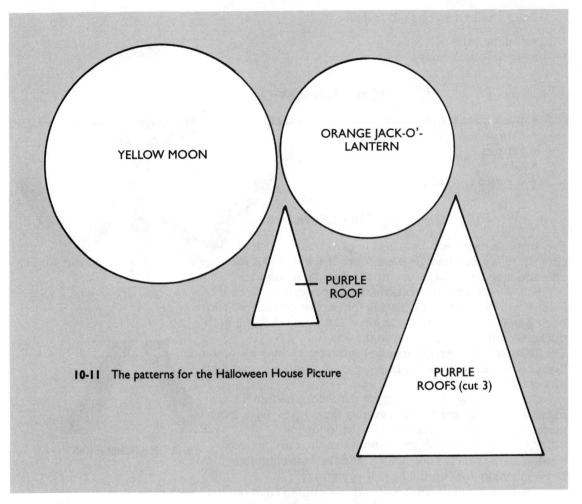

10-11 The patterns for the Halloween House Picture

(within image)
YELLOW MOON

ORANGE JACK-O'-LANTERN

PURPLE ROOF

PURPLE ROOFS (cut 3)

PUMPKIN LADY

A Pumpkin Lady made of shapes and letters! Can you imagine anything better? (FIG. 10-12).

Skills to Teach

Teach children 2 years old and up:

- The letters *I*, *V*, and *W*
- The colors *black*, *green*, and *orange*
- The *circle* and *triangle* shapes
- Gluing skills
- How many make *3*
- To count to *4* and *8*

Teach children 4 years old and up:

- Cutting skills
- Alphabetical order

Materials List

- Black, green, and orange construction paper
- Yarn, any color
- Scissors
- Glue
- A pencil and ruler

Directions

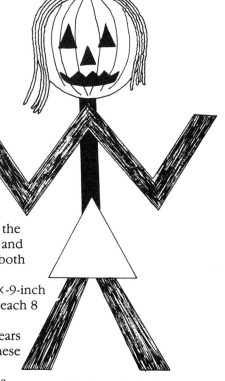

10-12 The Pumpkin Lady

Use the patterns in FIGS. 10-13 and 10-14 to trace an orange circle head, a green triangle dress, three black triangles for eyes and nose, and a black mouth for each Pumpkin Lady.

Fold a piece of black construction paper in half. Trace the letter *V* and the letter *W* by placing the pattern on the fold and tracing around it (FIG. 10-13). Cut these letters out through both thicknesses of paper, then unfold the letters.

To make the letter *I*, use pencil and ruler to draw a 1-×-9-inch black rectangle. To make the hair, cut eight pieces of yarn, each 8 inches long.

Cut everything out for younger children. Children 4 years old and up can do much of the cutting themselves. Give these pieces to the children and tell them the following:

"*A*. Glue the *three black triangles* on the *orange circle* head to make two eyes and a nose. Add the *black* mouth. Draw pumpkin lines on the head if you want to.

"*B*. Let's count the pieces of yarn." Count to *eight* out loud with each child. "How many pieces do you have? *Eight* pieces of yarn. Glue *four* pieces of yarn on one side of the Pumpkin Lady's head, and *four* pieces on the other side."

Help each child count four pieces of yarn. They can glue them in place by spreading glue on the head, then pressing the yarn into the glue.

"*C*. Glue the Pumpkin Lady's head on the end of the *black letter I*.

"*D*. Glue the *black letter W* below her chin to make arms.

"*E*. Turn the *black letter V* upside down and glue it on the other end of the *letter I* to make legs.

"*F*. Glue on the *green triangle* skirt."

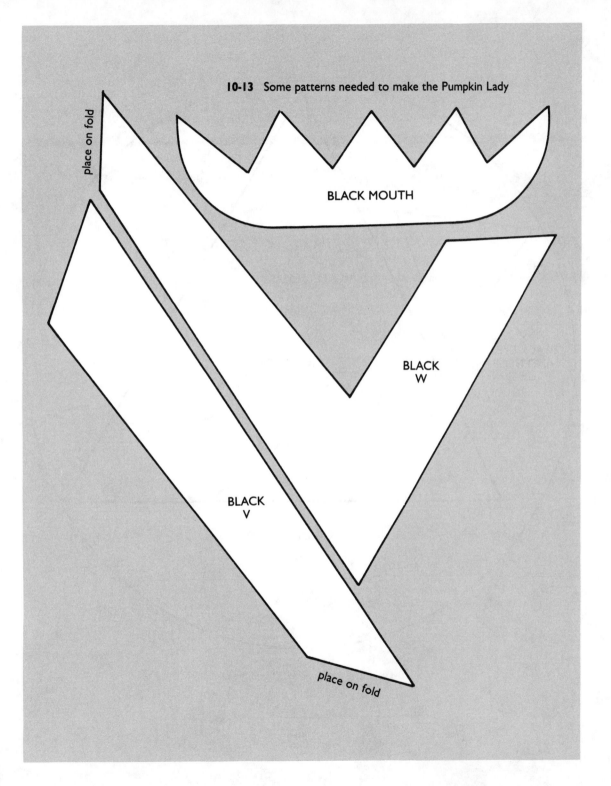

10-13 Some patterns needed to make the Pumpkin Lady

place on fold

BLACK MOUTH

BLACK
W

BLACK
V

place on fold

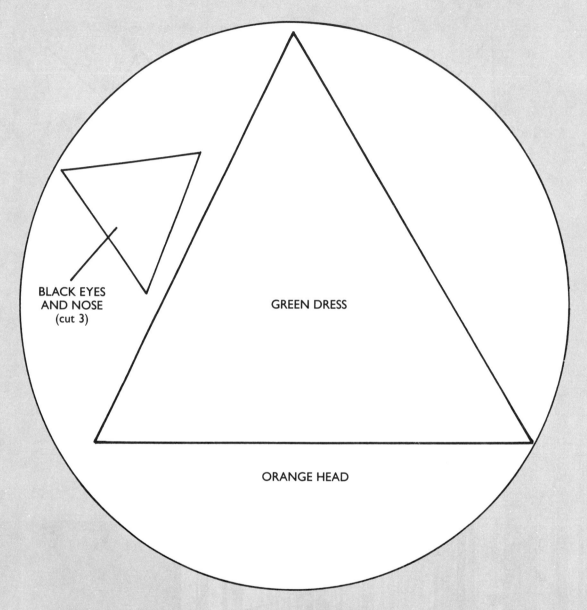

BLACK EYES
AND NOSE
(cut 3)

GREEN DRESS

ORANGE HEAD

10-14 More patterns for the Pumpkin Lady

TEN-CIRCLE PUMPKIN

Ten circles to make one pumpkin? How can that be? Try this craft and you will see! (FIG. 10-15).

Skills to Teach

Teach children 2 years old and up:

- The *circle* and *rectangle* shapes
- The colors *orange* and *green*
- Gluing skills
- To count to *10*

Teach children 4 years old and up:

- Cutting skills
- The meaning of *in half*

Materials List

- Orange and green construction paper
- Ruler and pencil
- Scissors
- Glue

10-15 The 10-Circle Pumpkin

Directions

Use the pattern in FIG. 10-16 to draw 10 orange circles and a green rectangle stem for each pumpkin. Draw a 2^1/2-inch slit or cut line in nine of the circles.

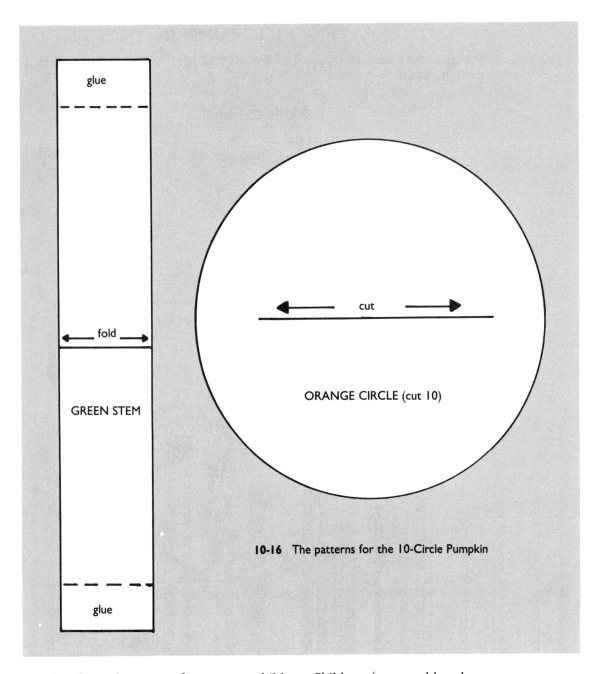

glue

fold

GREEN STEM

glue

cut

ORANGE CIRCLE (cut 10)

10-16 The patterns for the 10-Circle Pumpkin

Cut these shapes out for younger children. Children 4 years old and up should be encouraged to cut their own.

Using the cut line as a guide, cut a slit in nine of the circles.

Instruct your children by saying, "Let's see how many *orange circles* you have. Count them with me." Count the 10 circles out loud with each child. Then ask, "How many circles do you have? That's right, you have *ten*. *Ten* circles.

"Fold the *green rectangle in half* to make a pumpkin stem. Fold the glue line outward so the stem can be glued.

"Glue the *green rectangle* stem in the middle of the *orange circle* that does *not* have a slit.

"Hold each of the *orange circles* that are left so that the slit opens like a mouth. Slid each circle onto the circle that has the stem."

When the Ten-Circle Pumpkins are finished, they will stand by themselves.

BUY A PUMPKIN

This activity is a family tradition at our house. We cut the pumpkin outside when we can. When we can't, we use the kitchen table.

Skills to Teach

Teach children 2 years old and up:

- How to draw a face
- How to clean out a pumpkin
- What is in a pumpkin

Teach children 4 years old and up how to make a jack-o'-lantern.

Materials List

- Newspaper to cover the kitchen table
- A pumpkin for each child
- Black or purple water-based markers
- A sharp knife for you to use
- A big tablespoon

Directions

Take the children pumpkin-shopping. Let each child pick out his or her own pumpkin. Pumpkins are usually sold by the pound, so help them pick out ones in accordance with your budget.

Wipe the mud off the pumpkins when you return home. Spread thick layers of newspapers on a table, and set the pumpkins on them.

The children should choose the best side of their pumpkin. Then they can draw a face on it, using a water-based marker. The face does not have to be the traditional triangle-eyed jack-o'-lantern. They can draw any face they wish as long as it has two eyes, a nose, and a mouth. Two- and 3-year olds can draw very scary faces made only of circles!

Now it's your turn. Cut a large circle on the top of the pumpkin. Make a large V in the back of the pumpkin as part of the lid to show you how to put the lid back on.

Next, cut out the eyes, nose, and mouth as drawn by the child. Use a wet cloth or sponge to wipe away remaining traces of water-based marker.

Give the pumpkins back to the children. They can use a big tablespoon and their hands to scoop out the pulp and seeds. Use your knife to cut and scrape stubborn pulp so they can spoon it out. Cut the pulp from the inside of the lid.

When the jack-o'-lanterns are finished, ask the children to give you the seeds so they can be roasted.

A small warming candle can be set inside each jack-o'-lantern and lit, giving off an eerie glow. Supervise very closely, however. Blow out the candle after a few minutes of enjoyment, and never leave the child alone with the candle lit.

ROASTED PUMPKIN SEEDS

A delicious treat can be made from the seeds of all the pumpkins the children have carved.

Skills to Teach

Teach children 2 years old and up that pumpkin seeds can be cooked and eaten.

Materials List

- Seeds from 1 or more pumpkins
- 2 tablespoons cooking oil
- A jelly roll pan
- A wooden spoon
- Salt

Directions

Preheat oven to 350°F. Put the pumpkin seeds in a jelly roll pan that has sides on it. You do not have to remove all the pulp; just take away as much as you can.

Pour on 2 tablespoons cooking oil. Stir with a wooden spoon to coat all the seeds. Add more oil if necessary.

Roast in a 350°F oven for 40 minutes until the seeds begin popping and turn a golden brown.

Remove the seeds from the pan and drain on paper towels. Salt to taste. Serve hot or cold.

SPIDER BREAD

Spooky, spooky spider good to eat. I'll count his legs and nibble his feet! (FIG. 10-17).

10-17 Spider Bread

Skills to Teach

Teach children 2 years old and up:

- To sit still, listen, and follow directions
- How to measure, stir, and bake
- To be creative with dough

Materials List

- A large bowl and a wooden spoon
- $^1/_4$ cup warm water
- 1 package active dry yeast
- $^3/_4$ cup lukewarm water
- $^1/_3$ cup dry powdered milk
- $^1/_4$ cup sugar
- $^1/_4$ cup soft shortening
- 1 teaspoon salt
- One egg
- $3^1/_2$ cups flour

Directions

Help the children measure $^1/_4$ cup warm water into the large bowl. Add one package active dry yeast and stir until dissolved.

Help the children measure and add the remaining ingredients. They can take turns stirring the dough until it is mixed and smooth, or you can use an electric mixer with a dough hook and mix on slow speed for 2 minutes.

Cover the bowl with plastic wrap and let it rise in a warm place (85°F) for 1 hour.

Stir dough. Let it rise again, covered, for 30 minutes. Now it's ready to use.

Put aprons on the children, tied up high to keep flour off their tummies. Divide the dough into six equal pieces by cutting it with a knife. Give a piece to each child. Give the children a little pile of flour to keep their dough from sticking to the tabletop.

Tell the children to divide their dough into two equal pieces. One of these pieces is the body for the Spider. Put the body in the middle of a greased baking pan.

The children should divide their remaining lump of dough into eight pieces by pulling the dough apart, or by cutting it with a pizza cutter.

Tell them to roll each ball into a snake 4 inches long. Pinch each snake onto the Spider body. Cut or pull the tips off two legs. Stick the tips onto the Spider to make eyes.

Brush the Spiders with milk. Let them rise for 20 minutes. Bake at 400 °F for 12 to 15 minutes.

WITCH'S FINGERS

The longer and more crooked Witch's Fingers are, the better. It helps to have a smooth plastic cloth on your kitchen table for easy clean up.

Skills to Teach

Teach children 2 years old and up:

- How to work with dough
- How to measure, stir, and bake
- To count to 5
- How to print his or her own name

Materials List

- A large bowl
- A wooden spoon
- 1 1/2 cups warm water
- 1 package dry yeast
- 1 teaspoon salt
- 1 tablespoon sugar
- 5 cups flour
- One egg and 1 tablespoon water
- Coarse salt or table salt
- Paper plates and pencils

Directions

Preheat the oven to 350 °F. The children can grease two cookie sheets or jelly roll pans.

Help the children measure the warm water into the large bowl. Add the dry yeast. Let them stir it with a wooden spoon. Help them measure and stir in the salt, sugar, and flour. Count the cups of flour out loud with them as they add it to the bowl: "One . . . two . . . three . . . four . . . five. How many cups of flour did we add? *Five!*"

Shape the dough into a ball. Put a small pile of flour in front of each child, and let them smooth it around on the tabletop. Give each a portion of dough.

To make Witch's Fingers they should pull off a piece of dough the size of a walnut (or cut it off with a pizza cutter) and roll it between their hands until it is 15 inches long. They will need to hold it up in the air as they roll it to this length. Lay the Witch's Fingers on the greased baking sheets. Make sure they do not touch each other.

Put the egg and 1 tablespoon water in a jar with a tight-fitting lid. Shake hard. The children can brush this glaze on the Witch's Fingers, using a pastry brush. Sprinkle the Fingers with coarse salt or table salt.

Bake at 350 °F for 25 minutes. Loosen the Witch's Fingers from the pan with a metal spatula and separate them if necessary.

Give each child a paper plate and a pencil. Help each one write his or her name on the plate. Make sure they hold their pencils correctly and use uppercase and lowercase letters. Put each child's Witch's Fingers on his or her own plate to eat or to share.

Witch's Bones

Loosen the Witch's Fingers from the pan after they have baked. Separate them if necessary. Return them to the turned-off oven and leave them there until cool. They should be as hard and dry as the Witch's Bones in a few hours. Don't serve them to anyone who has weak teeth.

November

Turkey, pilgrim, and Indian crafts help the children learn Thanksgiving traditions. Throughout the chapter, emphasis is on teaching visual-motor skills that help coordinate the eye and finger muscles, following directions in sequence, and learning shapes, colors, and sizes.

Read-Your-Name Game

Play this game when giving the children paper plates for their cooking crafts, or paper cups for their drinks. Hold a plate or cup in front of you so everyone can see it.

Say, "I'm going to write someone's name on this plate (cup). If it is your name, raise your hand." Print a child's name on the plate or cup while spelling it out loud. "B−A−R−B−A−R−A. Whose name is this? That's right, Barbara. This is your plate (cup)." Give Barbara the plate or cup and repeat with the next child.

Some children will raise their hand for *every* plate or cup just to make sure they don't miss theirs. Eventually, though, they will learn to read not only their name, but also the names of all the other children present.

Craft-Training Skills to Learn

Preschool skills to practice in November include:

- Learning to recognize the colors and shapes
- Printing his or her name
- Drawing a face
- Counting to 10
- Stringing beads, another eye-hand coordination exercise
- Learning to cut, color, draw, and glue

CONSTRUCTION PAPER INDIAN

This Indian holds out his arms to me if I cut his clothes from a big letter *T*. (FIG. 11-1).

Skills to Teach

Teach children 2 years old and up:

- The colors *brown* and *red*
- The letters *T* and *X*
- Drawing and coloring skills
- Gluing skills
- How to write his or her name

Teach children 4 years old and up cutting skills.

Materials List

- Brown and red construction paper
- Ruler and pencil
- Scissors
- Glue
- Crayons
- Cellophane tape

11-1 The Construction Paper Indian

Directions

For each Indian, use the pencil and ruler to draw the letter *T* on a sheet of brown construction paper, as shown in FIG. 11-1. Draw a triangle 5^1/$_2$ inches tall at the bottom of the *T*, as shown. Give the T to your older child to cut out. You should do the cutting for the children under 4. *Do not* cut out the triangle at this time.

Use the pattern in FIG. 11-2 to trace a red circle head, two red hands, a brown feather, and two brown moccasins for each Indian. Cut these shapes out for your younger child, but encourage those over the age of 3 to cut their own.

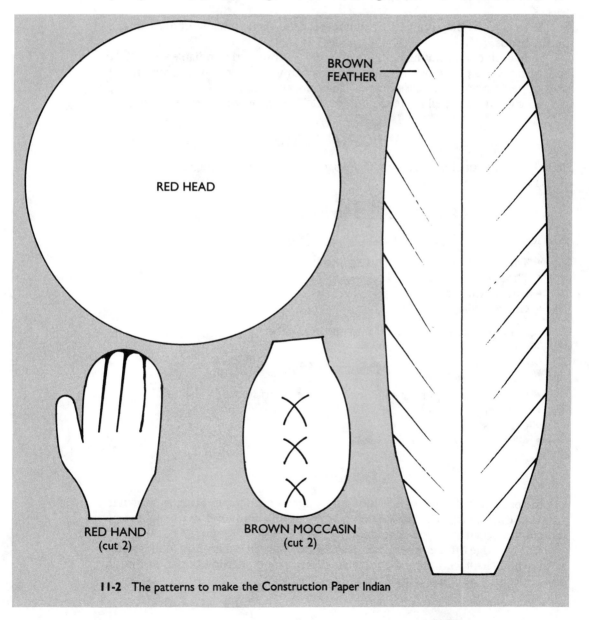

BROWN
FEATHER

RED HEAD

RED HAND
(cut 2)

BROWN MOCCASIN
(cut 2)

11-2 The patterns to make the Construction Paper Indian

Tell your children to snip the *brown letter T* all the way around with scissors to make the Indian's clothes look like buckskin. Then they should snip all the way around the *brown* feather slightly. Have cellophane tape ready if they snip too much and suddenly have two short feathers and half an Indian.

Tell them to use crayons to draw a headband, hair, and a face on the *red circle*. They should glue this Indian head to the top of the *brown letter T*. Then they can glue the two *red* hands on the crossbars of the *letter T*.

Help them cut out the *brown triangle*, forming two legs for the Indian. They can draw the *letter X* on the two moccasins, and glue them on the ends of the legs.

With crayons they can add a belt and beads to their Indian and draw fingers on the hands.

Help each child print his or her name on the front of the Indian's shirt. Make sure he holds his pencil or crayon correctly when writing or drawing, and that he uses uppercase and lowercase letters. If necessary, hold his hand lightly to help him do a good job. Spell his name out loud to him as he writes each letter.

PILGRIM MAN

To help teach your children about Thanksgiving, help them make this Pilgrim Man (FIG. 11-3).

Skills to Teach

Teach children 2 years old and up:

- The colors *white*, *black*, and *yellow*
- The *square* shape
- How to draw a face
- Gluing skills

Teach children 4 years old and up cutting skills.

Materials List

- 9-inch white paper plates. (Generic plates work well.)
- Scissors
- Crayons
- Glue

Directions

Use the pattern to draw a triangle along the edge of each paper plate, as shown in FIG. 11-3. Cut the triangle out for younger children. Children 4 years old and up can cut their own after you have drawn it.

Cut the edge off the paper plate, leaving two pilgrim collars 3$^{1}/_{2}$ inches wide, as shown in FIG. 11-3. This cut-off edging makes a cute pilgrim bonnet; just put it on a little girl's head like a headband.

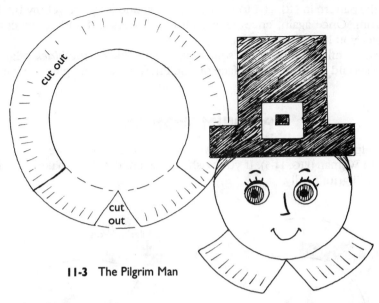

11-3 The Pilgrim Man

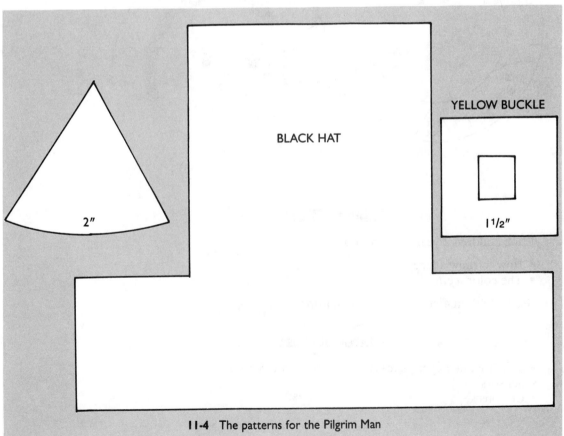

YELLOW BUCKLE

BLACK HAT

2"

1¹/₂"

11-4 The patterns for the Pilgrim Man

Use the pattern in FIG. 11-4 to trace a black hat and a square yellow buckle for each Pilgrim. Once again, encourage children 4 years old and up to cut these shapes after you have drawn them.

Tell your children to glue the *square yellow* buckle on the *black* pilgrim hat. Next they should draw hair and a face on the Pilgrim Man, and glue the hat on his head.

PILGRIM WOMAN

You can help the boys make the Pilgrim Man just described, while the girls make this Pilgrim Woman (FIG. 11-5). If you wish, all the children can make one of each, and have a Pilgrim family.

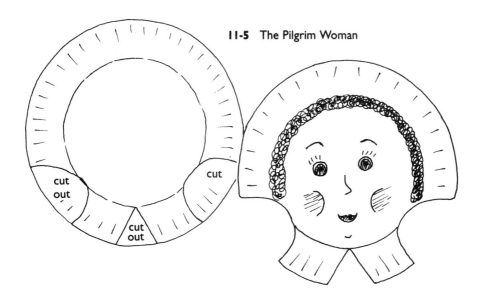

11-5 The Pilgrim Woman

Skills to Teach

Teach children 2 years old and up:

- How to draw a face
- The color *white*

Teach children 4 years old and up cutting skills.

Materials List

- 9-inch white paper plates (Generic plates work well.)
- Scissors
- Crayons

Directions

Use the pattern in FIG. 11-5 to draw a triangle and two rounded shapes along the edge of the paper plate for each Pilgrim Woman. Cut them out; children 4 years old and older can do their own cutting.

Your children can use crayons to draw a face and hair on the Pilgrim Woman. The top edge of the plate forms the woman's *white* hat. The two bottom edges form her *white* pilgrim collar.

_____ woolie-pullie_____

> Make masks from the Pilgrim Man and Pilgrim Woman by cutting out the eyes and tying a string to both sides of the paper plate face. Tie the mask over the child's face.

COFFEE CAN INDIAN DRUM

I just love my Indian Drum. I made it myself. It goes, "Thum, thum, thum." (FIG. 11-6).

Skills to Teach ·

Teach children 2 years old and up:

- The color *brown*
- To count to *10*
- Drawing skills
- Gluing skills

Teach children 4 years old and up how to cut paper *in half*.

Materials List

- Two 1-pound coffee cans
- Two plastic lids for each coffee can
- Brown construction paper
- Scissors
- Glue
- 10 dried beans for each can
- Cellophane tape
- Water-based markers

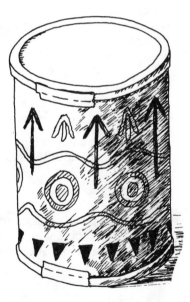

11-6 A Coffee Can Indian Drum

Directions

Use a can opener to remove both ends from each coffee can. Give each child two sheets of brown construction paper (use paper grocery bags as a substitute), scissors, glue, beans, and markers.

Help them cut one sheet of *brown* paper *in half* by folding it across the middle, opening it, and cutting along the fold mark. You do the cutting for children under the age of 4 unless you have a lot of brown paper to waste.

To make the papers look like animal skin, the children should crumple them up, and then straighten them out again. They should glue the half-sheet on their cans first, by spreading glue on the paper, and pressing it smoothly onto the can.

Help each child spread glue on the whole sheet of *brown* paper, and press it smoothly onto the rest of the can. The whole *brown* sheet will overlap the half-sheet, completely covering the can. Fold and glue the excess paper firmly inside both ends of the can.

Cover one end with a plastic lid. Now they are ready to put the 10 beans in their Indian Drums. Ask them to count the beans out loud with you as they drop them in. Then ask, "How many beans did you put in your drum? *Ten* beans."

Close each drum with the remaining lid. Tape both lids shut all the way around with cellophane tape to prevent the children from removing the beans.

They can decorate the Indian Drum with markers. The designs on the drum in FIG. 11-6 are authentic North American Indian signs.

CARDBOARD ROLL TOTEM POLE

Indians in the northwestern part of North America carved a wooden pole with emblems, or *totems*, that were important to their clan or family. The Cardboard Roll Totem Pole is made of authentic North American Indian designs (FIG. 11-7). Trace the designs, or let the children design their own "totems."

Skills to Teach

Teach children 2 years old and up coloring and gluing skills.
Teach children 4 years old and up:

- Tracing and cutting skills
- Facts about Indian totems

Materials List

- Paper towel cardboard rolls
- Three different colors of construction paper
- Water-based markers and crayons
- Scissors
- Glue

Directions

The children can trace the three totem patterns in FIGS. 11-8 and 11-9, or design their own totems.

Help them cut out the totems and color them. You must cut out the three totems for children younger than 4.

11-7 The Cardboard Roll Totem Pole

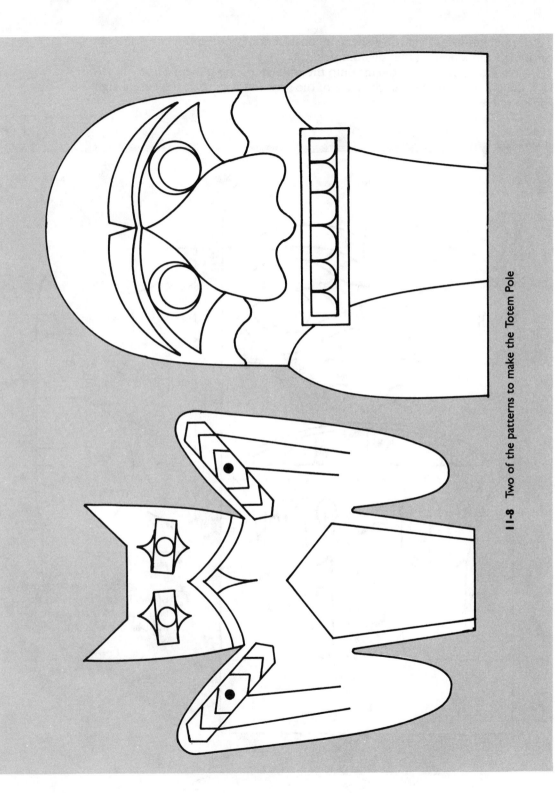

11-8 Two of the patterns to make the Totem Pole

Help them spread glue on a sheet of construction paper, and press it onto the cardboard roll, covering the roll completely.

Now they can glue the totems onto the roll, overlapping them a little. In FIG. 11-7, the top totem is glued to the back of the second totem to give it extra height and an interesting look.

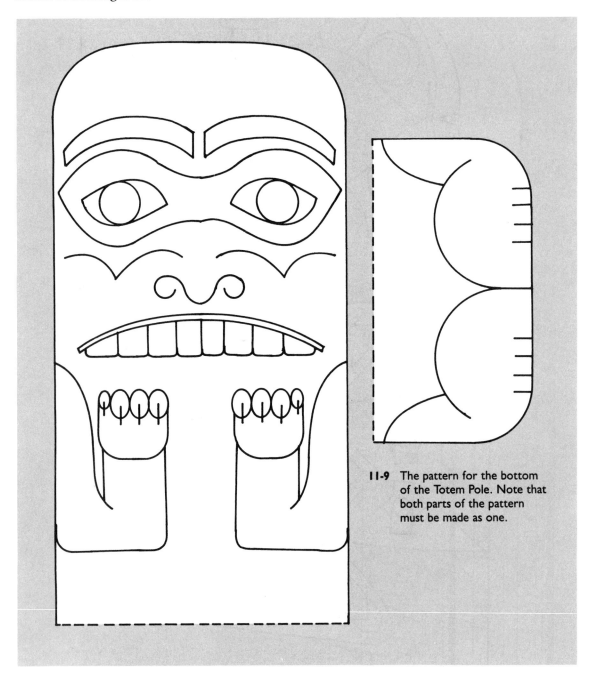

11-9 The pattern for the bottom of the Totem Pole. Note that both parts of the pattern must be made as one.

INDIAN BEADS

The children can dress up as Indians for Thanksgiving after they've made necklaces and bracelets of Indian Beads (FIG. 11-10). They'll have fun and learn at the same time.

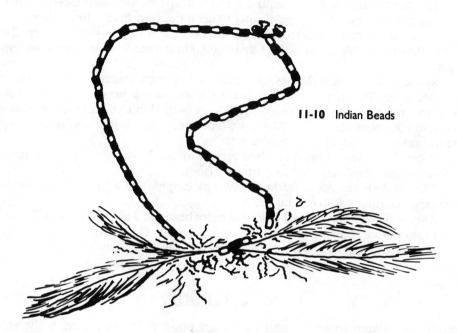

11-10 Indian Beads

Skills to Teach

Teach children 2 years old and up:

- The colors *red*, *blue*, *yellow*, and *green*
- How to string beads.

Materials List

- Short straight pasta called *chili macs* or *ditali*
- Red, blue, yellow, and green liquid food dye
- Four jars with lids
- Paper towels
- Two or three pipe cleaners for each child
- A piece of yarn 30 inches long for each child
- Feathers (marabou feathers from a craft store, or any others)
- Glue, *in a milk lid*

Directions

Divide the pasta among the four jars, filling each jar about one-third full. Pour a few drops of liquid food dye in the jars, a different color for each one. Put the lid on tightly.

Give these jars to the children to shake vigorously. The food dye will spread among all the little pasta pieces. If the lid comes off it will spread all over the children.

Open each jar and pour the colored pasta onto paper towels. Let them dry.

To string the Indian Beads, bend the end of a pipe cleaner and tie on the yarn. Squeeze it to the rest of the pipe cleaner to keep the yarn from falling off it.

Help the children tie one pasta on the other end of the yarn to keep the Indian Beads from falling off as they are strung. Put the beads where everyone can reach them.

As the children string the pasta beads onto their yarn, comment on the colors they are using. You might say, "Barbara, I see lots of *red* beads on your Indian necklace. You must like that color." Or, "Terry, why don't you add some *yellow* beads to your necklace?" Or, "Mary, the *blue* Indian beads that you're stringing are the same color as the shirt you're wearing."

When the children have filled their yarns with beads, remove the pipe cleaner and tie the yarn ends together to form necklaces.

The children can add a feather or two by dipping the end of the feather in glue, and inserting it into several beads.

They can make bracelets by stringing more beads on a pipe cleaner, and twisting it into a circle. Small children need only one pipe cleaner to fit around their wrist; larger children can twist two pipe cleaners together to make a larger bracelet.

CIRCLE TURKEY

Teach the children about the part the turkey plays in Thanksgiving, while you teach them colors and shapes. You can use the Circle Turkeys as decorations for your feast. (FIG. 11-11).

Skills to Teach

Teach children 2 years old and up:

- The colors *red*, *yellow*, *brown*, *orange*, and *black*
- The *circle* and *diamond* shapes
- Gluing skills

Teach children 4 years old and up:

- Cutting skills
- To follow directions

Materials List

- Red, yellow, brown, orange, and black construction paper
- Scissors
- Glue, *in a milk lid*
- Several feathers (Use marabou craft feathers or any others.)

11-11 The Circle Turkey

Directions

Use the pattern in FIG. 11-12 to draw five circles of graduated diameter in the colors suggested, or gather a variety of kitchen objects to trace around, each a little larger than the last. (The largest circle is not included in the pattern. It should be orange and approximately 7³/4 inches in diameter.) You could use a vitamin bottle lid, a drinking glass, a coffee cup, a sour cream container, a cereal bowl, and a large pot lid.

After you have drawn the circles, let the children cut them out. You must do the cutting for children under 4 years of age.

Use the patterns in FIGS. 11-12 and 11-13 to draw two black eyes, a yellow beak, two yellow feet, a red wattle, and a red neck for each turkey. Cut these shapes out or let the children do it. Then tell the children the following:

"*First*, glue the *brown circle* in the middle of the *largest orange circle*.

"*Second*, glue the *yellow circle* in the middle of the *brown circle*.

"*Third*, glue the *small orange circle* on the *yellow circle*.

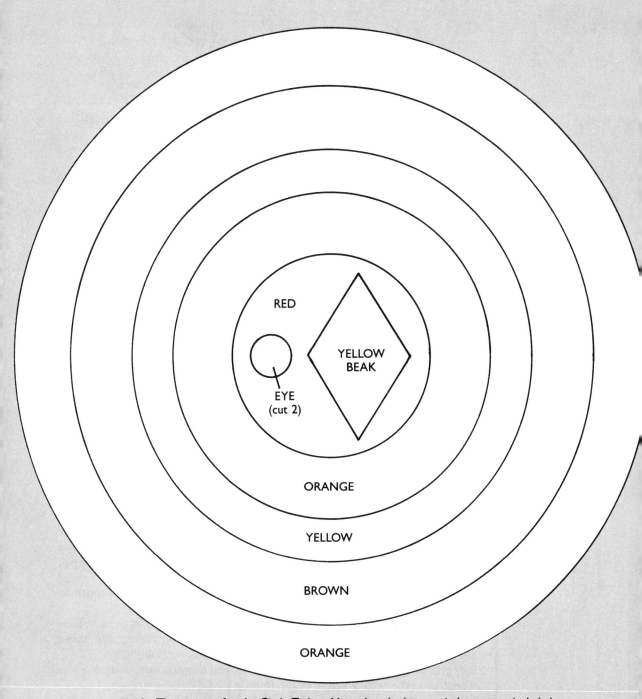

RED

YELLOW
BEAK

EYE
(cut 2)

ORANGE

YELLOW

BROWN

ORANGE

11-12 The patterns for the Circle Turkey. Note that the largest circles are not included.

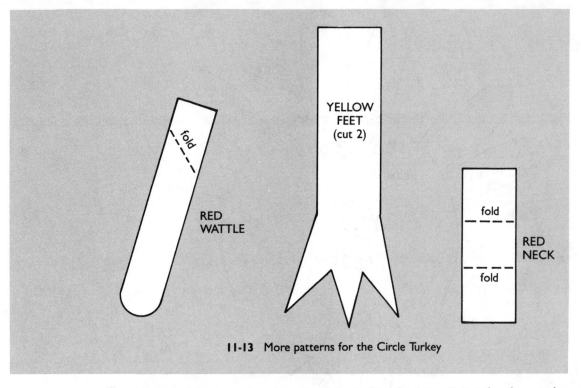

11-13 More patterns for the Circle Turkey

"*Fourth*, fold the *red* neck so that it looks like the *letter Z*. Put the glue on the two ends of the neck. Glue the neck in the middle of the *small orange circle*. Then glue the *red circle* head on the neck.

"*Fifth*, glue the two *little black circle* eyes on the *red circle* head. Fold the *yellow diamond* beak in half. Glue it below the *black circle* eyes.

"*Sixth*, glue the two *yellow* feet between the *brown circle* and the *large orange circle*.

"*Seventh*, dip some feathers in glue and *insert* them between the *brown circle* and the *large orange circle*."

TURKEY WITH PAPER FEATHERS

This turkey helps me draw and cut so fine. I also learn to count to nine! (FIG. 11-14).

Skills to Teach

Teach children 2 years old and up:

- The colors *yellow*, *brown*, *red*, and *orange*
- The *triangle* shape
- Gluing skills
- To count to *9*

Teach children 4 years old and up cutting skills.

11-14 The Turkey with Paper Feathers

Materials List

- Yellow, brown, red, and orange construction paper
- Construction paper in any other colors
- Scissors
- Glue

Directions

For each turkey, use the pattern in FIG. 11-15 to trace a brown head, a red wattle, two orange feet, an orange triangle beak, and nine feathers in any colors. Draw around a pot lid or bowl to make a $7^3/_4$-inch-diameter body with triangle wings drawn near the bottom; make this body yellow.

Cut out these shapes for younger children. Children 4 years old and up should be encouraged to cut their own.

Ask the children to count the turkey feathers out loud with you to see how many they have. After counting to nine with them, ask, "How many feathers do you have? You have *nine*."

Help the children glue the *nine* feathers on the back of the *yellow* turkey body. They should glue on the two *orange* feet and the *brown* turkey head, as shown in FIG. 11-14. Help them add the *orange triangle* beak.

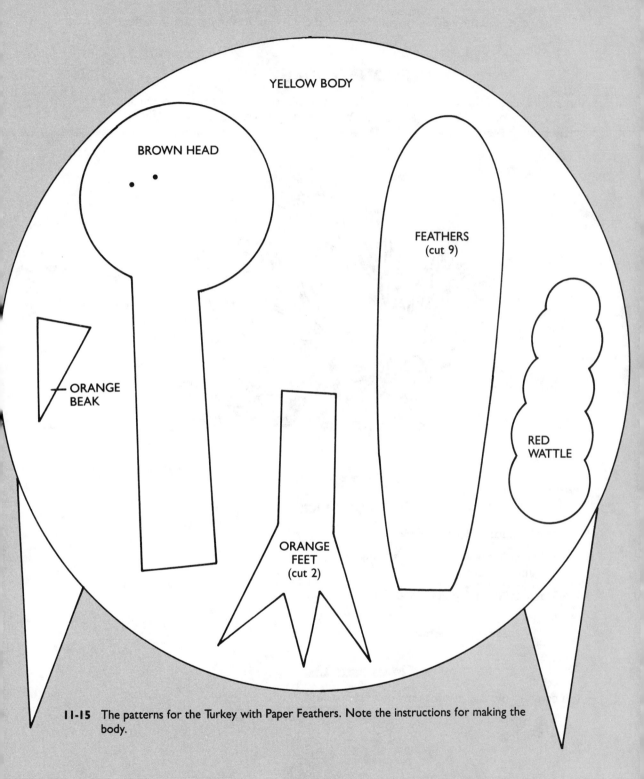

YELLOW BODY

BROWN HEAD

FEATHERS
(cut 9)

ORANGE
BEAK

RED
WATTLE

ORANGE
FEET
(cut 2)

11-15 The patterns for the Turkey with Paper Feathers. Note the instructions for making the body.

They can glue the *red* wattle on. Then each child can draw eyes on his or her turkey.

PINECONE TURKEY

Buy multicolored marabou feathers at the craft store, or use any feathers you can find for this Pinecone Turkey (FIG. 11-16). You can use them as centerpieces at your Thanksgiving Feast.

11-16 The Pinecone Turkey

Skills to Teach

Teach children 2 years old and up:

- The color *red*
- Gluing skills

Teach children 4 years old and up:

- Cutting skills
- The meaning of *wattle*

Materials List

You can buy the first three items in a craft store:

- Feathers
- Red felt

- Two paste-on movable eyes, size 4mm, for each turkey
- A pinecone 2 inches or bigger for each turkey
- Construction paper
- White glue, *in a milk lid*
- Scissors

Directions

Use the pattern provided in FIG. 11-17 to trace turkey feet onto construction paper. Trace a wattle for each turkey onto red felt. Cut these shapes out. Encourage children 4 years old and up to cut their own.

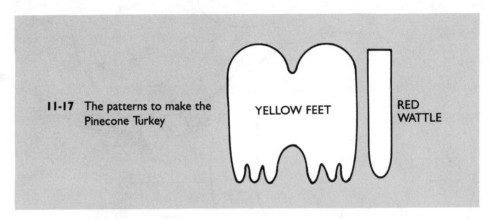

11-17 The patterns to make the Pinecone Turkey

YELLOW FEET

RED WATTLE

Give each child a pinecone, paper feet, a wattle, two eyes, and glue in a milk lid. Place the feathers where all the children can reach them.

Tell the children to turn the pinecone on its side, dip the end of each feather in glue, and stick it into the pinecone near the stem end. They can add as many feathers as they wish, depending on the size of the feathers.

On a real turkey the *wattle* is the fleshy red piece that hangs down over the turkey's beak. Help the children glue the *red* felt wattle to the side of the pinecone tip so that the tip looks like the turkey's beak.

Next they should glue the eyes, one on each side of the turkey's beak. Put lots of glue on the paper feet and stick them to the bottom of each turkey so they will stand up or set each turkey in the gluey milk lid. Let them dry all day or overnight.

If, despite their feet, the turkeys tip over because of their heavy tail, glue their feet to a piece of cardboard and pretend it's a barnyard. The children can draw corn and a water trough for their turkeys on the cardboard. You could also lean the turkey against something.

PAPER PLATE TURKEY

Paper Plate Turkey is a very cute fellow. He stands right up to teach *red* and *yellow*. (FIG. 11-18).

11-18 The Paper Plate Turkey

Skills to Teach

Teach children 2 years old and up:

- The colors *red* and *yellow*
- The *triangle* shape
- Coloring skills
- To count to 5

Teach children 4 years old and up cutting skills.

Materials List

- Two 9-inch white paper plates for each turkey. (Buy generic; they make good crafts.)
- Red and yellow construction paper
- Metal paper fasteners

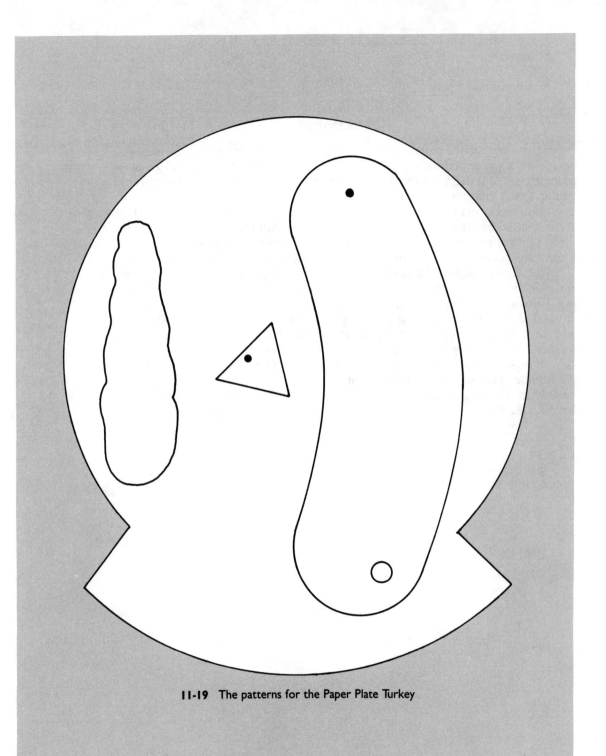

11-19 The patterns for the Paper Plate Turkey

- Five marabou craft feathers or other feathers for each turkey
- Scissors
- Glue, *in a milk lid*
- Crayons and a pen

Directions

For each turkey, use the pattern in FIG. 11-19 on p. 209 to draw the turkey head and body on the paper plate. On construction paper, trace a red wattle and a yellow triangle beak. Cut them out for the younger child; encourage children 4 years old and up to cut their own.

Use a pen to draw the turkey's feathers, feet, and eyes, as shown in FIG. 11-19. Your children can color the turkey head and body with crayons.

Tell them to glue the *yellow triangle* on the turkey's head to make a beak. Then they can glue the *red* wattle over the beak so that the wattle hangs down.

Help them fasten the turkey's head to its body with the paper fastener. They can glue on the *five* feathers by dipping them in the glue one at a time, and sticking them on the front of the turkey's body.

Ask them, ''How many feathers did you glue on the turkey? Let's count them and find out.'' Count the feathers out loud with them. Then ask, ''How many feathers? *Five* feathers on your turkey.''

To make the Paper Plate Turkey stand up, cut a rectangle 3 × 4 inches from the middle of the second paper plate. In the center of this rectangle cut a vertical slit 2^1/$_2$ inches long. Fold the rectangle horizontally. Insert the bottom of the turkey into the slit.

December

Christmas crafts wrap up the year and this book. Many of the crafts, such as the tree ornaments, are suitable for gifts, but my favorite is the Holly Leaf Napkin Rings. A set of them makes a beautiful gift for a special friend or teacher. If you cut the felt, even the youngest child can help glue them together.

A Sweet Ornament

The Sweet Gum Ornament has nothing to do with chewing gum. The Sweet Gum is a shade tree found in the eastern United States. It has star-shaped leaves with five to seven points on them, and it turns a lovely scarlet and gold color in the fall.

If you're lucky enough to live near one, or if you know someone who does, collect *gum balls*, the dark brown spiny seed pods that fall off the tree in autumn. Store them in a paper bag until they dry. Don't put them in plastic or they will mold.

A few years ago my children and I traveled with my husband to a business conference in New Jersey. There were Sweet Gum trees all around the tennis courts at the conference center. The children gathered the fattest gum balls and we brought them home to Illinois in a hotel laundry bag. The locals thought we were crazy, but at Christmastime we had enough gum balls for a whole Brownie troop to make ornaments.

Craft-Training Skills to Learn

The Sweet Gum Ornament not only looks nice, it also provides a good lesson in visual discrimination as the children try to find every little hole in the seed pod. It also provides practice in eye-hand coordination as they stick a glue-coated toothpick in the tiny hole.

Other Craft-training skills to practice while preparing for Christmas include:

- Following directions
- Learning the meaning of *first* through *seventh*
- Learning the meaning of *above*, *below*, *inside*, and *close together*
- How to fringe and to tie a knot
- How to use tape and glitter
- Recognizing the colors and shapes
- Putting things together
- How to cut and glue
- How to write "Merry Christmas"

SANTA CALENDAR

Pull off a ring every night until you reach the beard of white! (FIG. 12-1).

Skills to Teach

Teach children 3 years old and up:

- How to count to *24*
- Number recognition of *1* through *24*
- How to write numbers
- How to make a paper chain

Materials List

- 9-inch white paper plate
- Red, green, blue, and black construction paper
- Cotton balls or polyester stuffing (Fabric stores sell large bags of stuffing.)
- Paper punch
- Scissors
- Glue
- A pen for writing numbers

12-1   The Santa Calendar

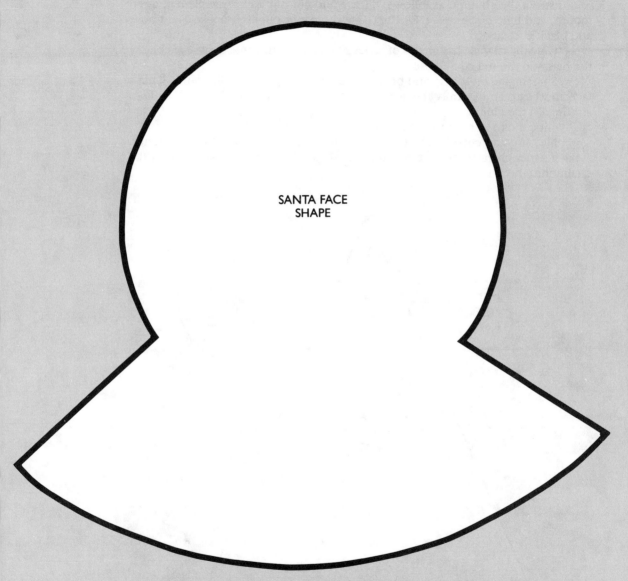

I2-2 The pattern for the Santa Calendar

Directions

Use the pattern in FIG. 12-2 to trace a Santa face shape onto the paper plate. Cut this out. You will need to prepare the pieces of the craft for younger children. Show children 4 years old and up how to trace and cut the pieces themselves.

Instruct the children as follows: "Trace and cut out a red triangle hat, a red mouth, and blue circle eyes (FIG. 12-3). Use the paper punch to make a red nose and black eyeballs.

"Glue the triangle hat on top of Santa's head. Glue the blue circle eyes below the hat. Add the red circle nose.

"Spread glue on the tip and brim of the hat. Also put glue all around Santa's face and beard so that only the eyes and nose are left. Now stick cotton balls or stuffing on the glue.

"Glue the mouth on top of the cotton beard.

"Measure and cut 12 red strips and 12 green strips that are $3/4 \times 8$ inches. Make a paper chain from the red and green strips. Glue or staple one end of the chain onto the Santa face.

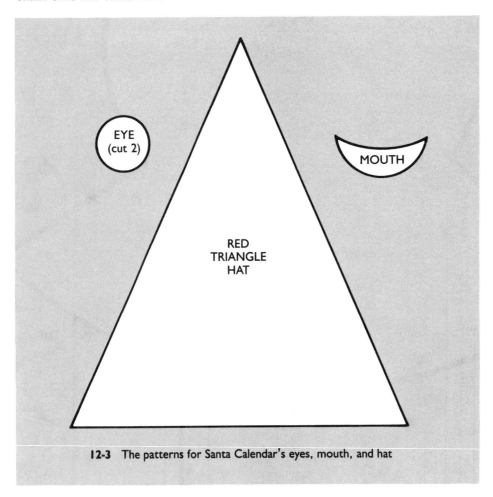

12-3 The patterns for Santa Calendar's eyes, mouth, and hat

"Use a pen or narrow marker to write the number *1* on the loop farthest from the face. Write number *2* on the next loop up. Continue writing until each loop has a number.

"At bedtime on December 1, tear off loop number *1*. Tear off one loop each night. When you reach loop number *24*, it will be Christmas Eve! Remember to leave cookies and milk for Santa, and carrots for the reindeer."

GROCERY SACK RUDOLPH

A delightful Christmas decoration is this Grocery Sack Rudolph, which can be made with simple materials. (FIG. 12-4).

Skills to Teach

Teach children 2 years old and up:

- The *rectangle*, *circle*, and *triangle* shapes
- The colors *red*, *white*, *brown*, and *black*
- Gluing skills
- The meaning of *close together* and *on top of*

Teach children 4 years old and up:

- Cutting skills
- How to fringe

Materials List

- A large brown grocery sack for each Rudolph
- A pencil and ruler
- White typing paper
- Black and red construction paper
- Glue
- Scissors
- Cotton balls (optional)

12-4   The Grocery Sack Rudolph

Directions

Using a pencil and ruler, measure and draw a triangle 12 × 14 × 14 inches on the plain side of each grocery sack, and cut them out.

For each child, use the pattern provided in FIG. 12-5 to draw and cut two antlers from the remainder of the grocery sack.

Trace and cut out two black rectangle eyelashes, two black circle eyeballs, two white eyes, and a red nose for each child. Encourage children 4 years old and up to do their own cutting.

Give the cutout pieces to the children and tell them the following:

"*First*, glue the *red circle* nose onto the point of the *brown triangle*.

"*Second*, glue the *white circle* eyes *close together* near the middle of the *triangle*. Glue the *black circle* eyeballs *on top of* the *white* eyes.

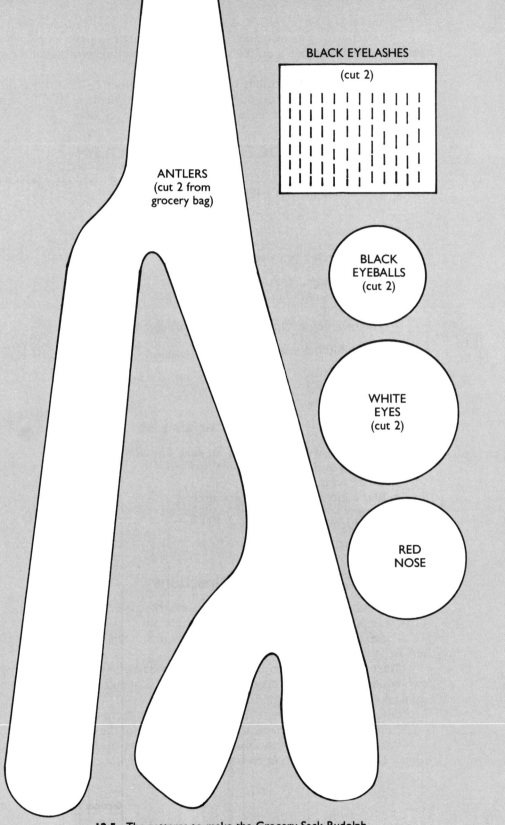

BLACK EYELASHES
(cut 2)

ANTLERS
(cut 2 from
grocery bag)

BLACK
EYEBALLS
(cut 2)

WHITE
EYES
(cut 2)

RED
NOSE

12-5 The patterns to make the Grocery Sack Rudolph

"*Third, fringe* the *black rectangle* eyelashes. Make them curl up by carefully wrapping the fringes around a pencil.

"*Fourth,* glue the *black* eyelashes on the eyes so that the eyes are partly covered.

"*Fifth,* glue the two *brown* antlers *on top of* Rudolph's head."

If you wish, add a skinny red triangle hat 11 inches tall and 5^1/$_2$ inches wide at its base. Glue cotton balls along the brim of the hat. Glue tufts of cotton on both sides of the hat's pointed top. The weight of the cotton will make the top of the hat fall forward into Rudolph's face.

REINDEER GOODY BAG

This is the perfect party take-home bag for cookies, toys, and candy (FIG. 12-6).

Skills to Teach

Teach children 2 years old and up:

- The *oval* and *circle* shapes
- The meaning of *below*
- How to draw a mouth
- How to write his or her name

Teach children 5 years old and up:

- Tracing and cutting skills

Materials List

- A 5^1/$_2$-×-3^1/$_8$-×10^3/$_4$-inch plain brown lunch bag
- Black and white construction paper
- A ^{1}/$_2$-inch red pompom
- Scissors
- Glue
- Black marker
- Paper punch
- Two notebook reinforcers
- Red and green tissue wrapping paper
- 18-inch narrow red ribbon

12-6 The Reindeer Goody Bag

Directions

Place the antler pattern (FIG. 12-7) at the top of the flat lunch bag. Show the children 5 years old and up how to trace around the pattern and cut it out through all thicknesses of the bag. Do this step ahead of time for younger children.

Help the children punch a hole in the front and back of the bag. Cover the holes with notebook reinforcers. Help the children tie on a ribbon handle.

They can use the patterns to trace two *white oval* eyes and two *black circle* eyeballs. Tell them to glue these on the bag, *below* the antler cut.

The children can glue on a red pompom nose. Then they can draw a mouth with the black marker *below* the nose.

Help them write their name *below* the mouth. Hold their hands lightly if necessary to help them print neatly.

Next the children can cut red and green tissue paper into 1/8-×-6-inch strips. They can put a handful of strips in their Reindeer Goody Bag as a nest for party favors.

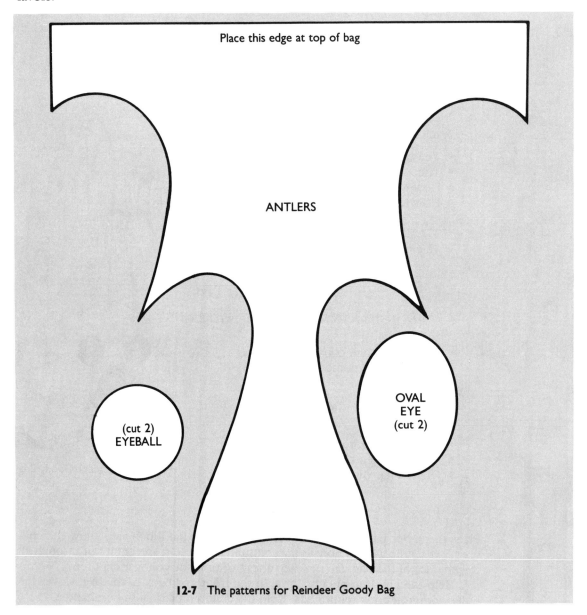

Place this edge at top of bag

ANTLERS

(cut 2)
EYEBALL

OVAL
EYE
(cut 2)

12-7 The patterns for Reindeer Goody Bag

SEED AND CONE MENORAH

Each child can celebrate Hanukkah by making a menorah to light on the last day of the holiday (FIG. 12-8).

Skills to Teach

Teach children 4 years old and up:

- The *rectangle* shape
- How to count to *8*
- The meaning of the menorah

Materials List

- Pencil
- Ruler
- Scissors
- Blue or white poster board
- Paper cup and popsicle stick
- White glue
- 1/4 cup birdseed
- Eight 2 1/4-inch birthday candles
- One 3 1/2-inch birthday candle
- A pinecone soaking in a bowl of water

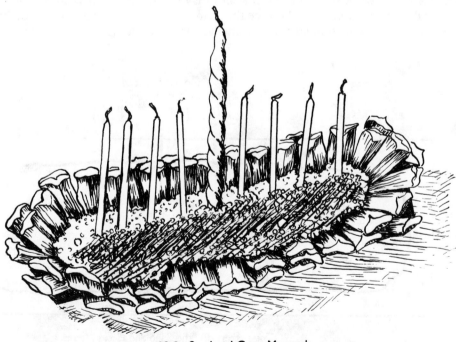

12-8 Seed and Cone Menorah

Directions

Use the pencil, ruler, and scissors to measure and cut out a rectangle 2 × 6 inches from the poster board. Children 5 years old and up can do some of the measuring and cutting themselves.

Help the child measure 1/4 cup birdseed into a paper cup. Next, he should add one tablespoon white glue to the birdseed. Tell him to stir the seed and glue together until well mixed.

The child should use the popsicle stick to mound the seed-glue mixture into an elongated oval down the middle of the rectangle. Use the pattern in FIG. 12-9 as an aid. This is a very sticky mixture that will cling to fingers; use the popsicle stick to scrape, shape, and smooth the seed. Tell the child the following directions:

"Insert the larger birthday candle in the center of the seed mound. This is the *shammes*, or leader, candle which will be used to light the others. On each side of the shammes, insert four small candles. Use the popsicle stick to push and smooth the seed around each candle.

"After five minutes, gently twist and remove the shammes. It will be replaced in the menorah after the craft has completely dried. Allow the menorah to dry for 2 days.

"While it is drying, pull apart the pinecone that has been soaking in water. Grab the bottom scales between forefinger and thumb and pull downward, one scale at a time. Let them dry.

"Spread a line of glue on the cardboard, around the base of the seed mound. Lay the pinecone scales in the glue with the rounded edge pointed outward. Position them close together to completely cover the cardboard. Add more glue if the scales seem loose. A second layer of scales may be added if you wish. Let your menorah dry for several days. Replace the shammes in the center of the menorah. Light this with the help of an adult on the last day of Hanukkah."

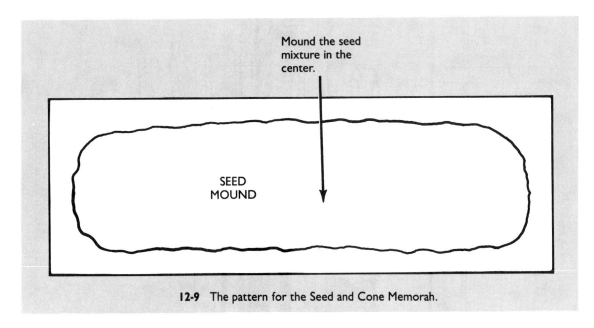

Mound the seed mixture in the center.

SEED MOUND

12-9 The pattern for the Seed and Cone Memorah.

SWEET GUM ORNAMENT

The finished Sweet Gum Ornament looks like the sphere the baby was placed in for his trip to Earth in the movie *Superman* (FIG. 12-10). It makes a unique tree ornament that will stick by itself in the tree branches. No hook or ribbon is needed.

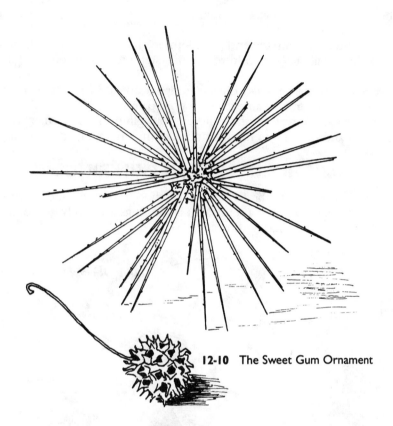

12-10 The Sweet Gum Ornament

Skills to Teach

Teach children 2 years old and up:

- To follow directions
- Eye-hand coordination
- Visual discrimination
  (The child must find every hole in the gum ball.)
- The meaning of *insert*

Materials List

- Gum balls from a Sweet Gum tree
- A box of round wooden toothpicks

- White glue, in a milk lid
- Old newspapers
- Gold spray paint
- Glitter, any color

Directions

Give the children the gum balls and some toothpicks. Pour a small amount of glue into a milk lid for each child.

Tell the children to dip the end of a toothpick into the glue and *insert* it into a hole in the gum ball. They should repeat this step until every hole is filled with one toothpick.

Now it's your turn. Spread old newspapers outside or on the floor of the garage. Spray the ornaments all over with gold paint.

While the paint is wet, let the children pour glitter on the ornaments. Shake off the excess and return it to its container. Let the ornaments dry overnight.

SIX HOLLY LEAF NAPKIN RINGS

This craft requires a trip to the fabric or craft shop to buy red and green felt. It's included in this book because a set of six napkin rings is a lovely gift for a child to make and give for Christmas (FIG. 12-11).

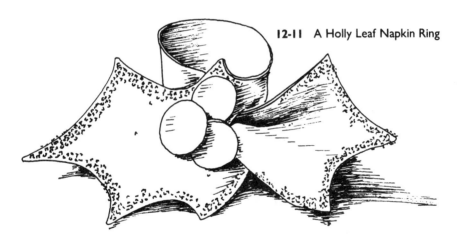

12-11   A Holly Leaf Napkin Ring

Skills to Teach

Teach children 2 years old and up:

- How many make *3*
- The *circle* shape
- Gluing skills
- Assembling skills
- How to use glitter

Teach children 8 years old and up cutting skills.

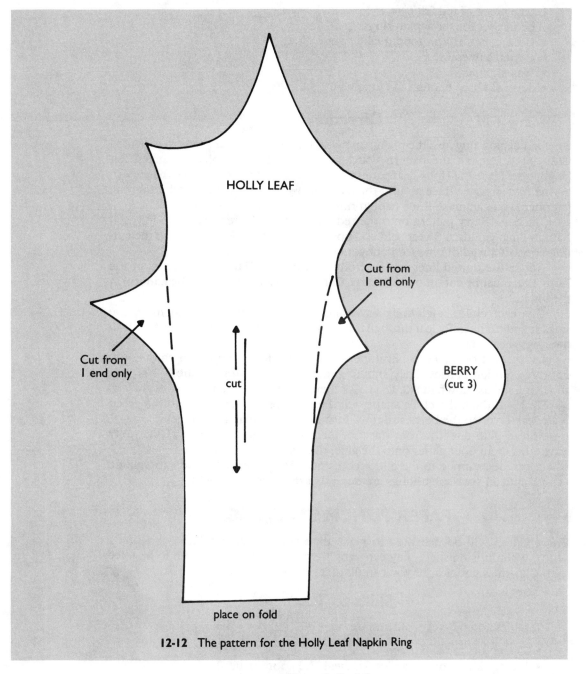

HOLLY LEAF

Cut from
I end only

Cut from
I end only

cut

BERRY
(cut 3)

place on fold

12-12 The pattern for the Holly Leaf Napkin Ring

Materials List

- Plain paper and a pencil
- Two pieces of $8^{3}/_{4}$-×-$11^{3}/_{4}$-inch green felt for six napkin rings

- One piece of red felt $8^3/4$-×-$11^3/4$-inches or smaller for six napkin rings
- Contact cement or good-quality white glue
- Glitter, any color
- Waxed paper
- Scissors sharp enough to cut felt

Directions

For each napkin ring, use the plain paper and pencil to trace the pattern provided (FIG. 12-12). Cut out the pattern you have made. Fold one piece of green felt lengthwise. Place the Holly Leaf pattern on the felt, with the flat end of the pattern on the folded edge. Trace around the pattern. If you cut carefully and refold the felt once, you can make three napkin rings from each piece of felt.

Trace the Berry pattern onto the red felt. Cut out 18 red berries; 3 for each Napkin Ring. Children 8 years old and up can cut the felt themselves. Do the cutting yourself ahead of time for younger children.

Notice the dotted lines on the Holly Leaf pattern. These two pieces of the Holly Leaf must be cut off one leaf only. Cut a 1-inch slit (shown on the pattern) in the big leaf.

Give each child six felt holly leaves and 18 red felt berries. Help them slip the smaller end of the holly leaf through the 1-inch slit, forming a ring. Repeat until all the rings are made.

Lay a sheet of waxed paper under one Napkin Ring. Help each child count out three red felt berries. They should glue them onto the larger holly leaf, just above the slit, as shown in FIG. 12-11. Ask them what shape the red berries are (*circle*). To teach them the circle shape, tell them to glue the *circles* onto the green holly leaf. Overlap the berries slightly, forming a triangular arrangement.

Spread glue directly from the tube or bottle along the edges of the holly leaves. Let them pour glitter onto the glue; the waxed paper will catch the excess, which can be returned to the glitter container. Gently shake off the extra glitter. Repeat until all six Napkin Rings are done. Let them dry overnight.

PAPER PUNCH STOCKING

The children will be delighted to make their own Paper Punch Stocking (FIG. 12-13). When it is finished, they can hang them up and wait for them to be filled with Christmas goodies, or you can fill them right away.

Skills to Teach

Teach children 2 years old and up:

- The colors *red* and *green*
- Lacing skills (good practice for eye-hand coordination)
- Drawing skills
- How to write his or her name

Teach children 6 years old and up cutting skills.

Materials List

- Red and green construction paper
- Scissors
- A paper punch
- A 72-inch piece of red or white or green yarn for each stocking
- A pipe cleaner for each stocking
- Crayons or water-based markers

Directions

For each child, draw a stocking shape on one sheet of construction paper, as shown in FIG. 12-13. The stocking should be 6 1/2 inches wide at the top and 12 inches long. Draw a rounded heel and toe.

Cut the stocking shape out of both red and green paper by holding the two sheets together and cutting them as one. Encourage children 6 years old and up to cut their own.

Continue holding the two pieces together. Use the paper punch to make holes 1 inch apart around the edges of the stocking. Do not punch holes along the top of the stocking.

12-13   A Paper Punch Stocking

Tie a 72-inch piece of yarn to the end of a pipe cleaner. Twist the pipe cleaner back on itself to hold the yarn.

Give two paper stockings and the yarn to each child. Tell them to lace the *red* and *green* stocking shapes together, starting at the top and lacing all the way around.

Then they can decorate the stockings with crayon or marker drawings. They should print their names neatly at the top, using uppercase and lowercase letters.

Fill the stocking with candy and small toys, or with a small box of crayons and paper.

CYLINDER CANDLE

A candle to make, so pretty to see, teaches five shapes in steps one, two, and three! (FIG. 12-14).

Skills to Teach

Teach children 2 years old and up:

- The *rectangle*, *cylinder*, *square*, *triangle*, and *circle* shapes
- The colors *red*, *white*, and *yellow*
- How to glue
- How to follow directions

Materials List

- Red construction paper, cut into a 7-×-11-inch rectangle
- White tissue wrapping paper, cut into a 7-inch square
- A paper towel roll
- Yellow water-based marker
- A small plastic lid to use as a base for the finished candle
- Glue
- Scissors
- Ruler
- Pencil
- Items to decorate candle, such as lace, ribbon, or holly (optional)

Directions

Tell the children to spread glue on the *red rectangle*. They can wrap the rectangle around the *cylinder* to cover it. This is the candle.

Tell the children to color the *white* tissue paper *square* with the *yellow* marker. Help them fold it into a *triangle*. Help them put glue on one corner of the triangle. Then they should stick it into one end of the cylinder and push about half of the triangle in.

To make the tissue look like a flame, pinch it up into a point. Now the candle is lit.

Help them glue a small plastic lid, such as the one that covers canned peanuts, on the bottom of the candle. Older children can decorate their candle with glitter, lace, ribbon, or holly.

CANDY CANE ELEPHANT

The Candy Cane Elephant makes a delightful tree ornament or holiday decoration (FIG. 12-15).

12-14 The Cylinder Candle

Skills to Teach

Teach children 2 years old and up:

- The color *red*
- Gluing skills
- How to use tape
- How to draw a face
- How to tie a knot

Teach children 4 years old and up:

- Tracing and cutting skills
- How to write ''Merry Christmas''

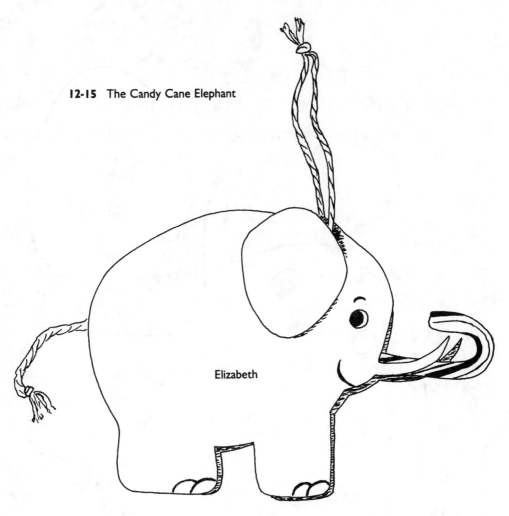

Elizabeth

Materials List

- A plain sheet of paper and a pencil for each elephant
- Red construction paper
- A pen
- Scissors
- Glue
- Yarn
- Transparent tape
- A paper punch
- 2$\frac{1}{2}$-inch candy canes, one for each elephant

Directions

Use the pattern in FIG. 12-16 to trace the elephant and his ears onto the plain paper. Cut them out and use them as patterns.

EARS (cut 2)

12-16 The patterns for the Candy Cane Elephant

For each elephant, fold a piece of red construction paper lengthwise. Lay the pattern on the paper with the top of the elephant's back along the fold. Trace the elephant and two ears.

Cut them out, being careful not to cut the fold. Children 4 years old and up can do their own tracing and cutting, with a little help from you.

Use the paper punch to punch a hole through both sides of the elephant's head. Show your children how to insert a 12-inch piece of yarn through this hole, and how to tie it in a knot to form a loop.

Cut a 4-inch piece of yarn for the tail. Help your children tie a knot near one end. They can tape the other end inside the elephant card so most of the yarn sticks out. Then they can separate the strands of yarn on the end of the tail to make a tassel.

Show them where to draw the eyes, mouth, and toes. They can print their names on the front of the elephant, and "Merry Christmas" inside the card. As they draw and write, be sure that they hold the pens correctly. Spell the words out loud to them as they write each letter. Make sure they use uppercase and lowercase letters where they are needed.

Now they can glue one ear on each side of the elephant's head, covering the punched hole. Help them tape the candy cane inside the card, letting it stick out as a trunk. They can hang the Candy Cane Elephant on a door knob or on the Christmas tree.

NO-COOK PEANUT BUTTER/HONEY BALLS

The final project is a candy that can be made especially for Christmas, or any time for a treat.

Skills to Teach

Teach children 2 years old and up:

- To sit still, listen, and follow directions
- How to work with dough
- How to write his or her first and last name

Materials List

- Paper plates and pencils
- A large bowl and wooden spoon
- 1 cup peanut butter
- 1 cup honey
- 2½ cups dry powdered milk

Directions

Give each child a paper plate. Tell them to turn the plate upside down and to print their first and last names on it. Help each child by spelling the name out loud as he or she writes it. "Your name is spelled *M . . . A . . . R . . . Y*, Mary."

Help the children measure the peanut butter, honey, and dry powdered milk into the bowl. Let everyone takes turns stirring until the ingredients are well blended.

Spoon a portion of dough onto each child's paper plate. The children can eat it all themselves and get a tummy ache, or they can roll it into bite-sized balls to share with the family after supper.

Refrigerate the paper plates with the candy on it for 30 minutes. This candy is even better the next day, but it probably won't last until then.

Index